Language Triathlon for Peacemakers

TO

FROM

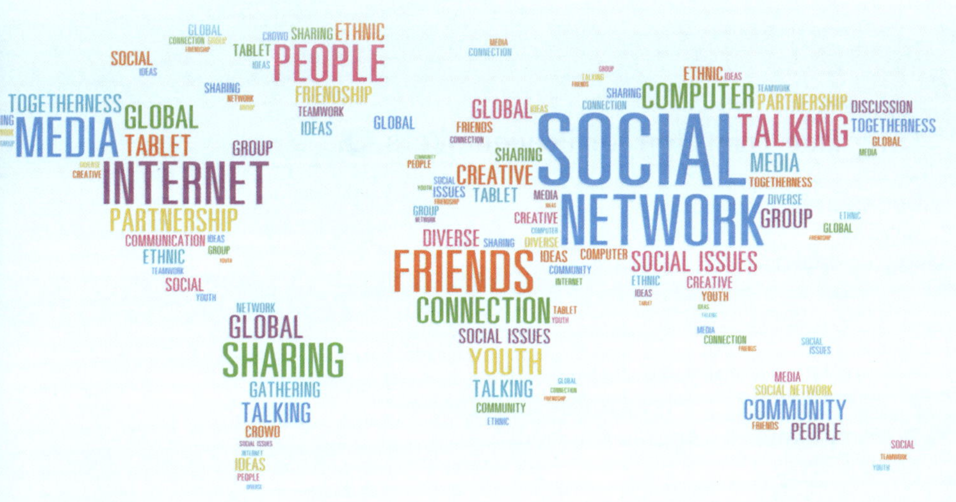

Language Triathlon for Peacemakers 1

Dongmin Kim
Jiayi Xu
Kayo Nonaka

ISBN: 978-89-318-1644-0

NACHIMVAN (COMPASS) Publising Co.
B 1607 Blue9 Bldg.
583 Yang Chun-ro Gangseo-Gu Seoul
Korea 07547

www.nabook.net

PRINTED IN KOREA

LEVINE LANGUAGE CENTER

피스메이커를 위한 4개 국어 성구 33

Dongmin Kim

Jiayi Xu

Kayo Nonaka

나침반

Foreword

East Asia has a long history of military conflicts and distrust. Those conflicts and distrust have always been involved in the history of East Asia. Efforts to create peace in the region are often laughed at by the lack of willingness to lower cultural and political barriers. Working to create peace in East Asia has never been taken seriously because the history of politics and culture have not changed much.

I read in the news every day that political problems in East Asia, such as fighting for land, still continue. From the looks of it, the idea of war is not hard to believe.

As a Christian, I believe that Christianity and communication on a personal level are very important, particularly in East Asia, where the informal process, guānxì/kankei/gwangye, is important. Christ said, "Blessed are the peacemakers, for they will be called children of God." (Matthew 5:9). Peacemaking is not passive but active, so taking "action" is a must. Learning different languages is an important part of sharing culture. Through this sharing we can commit to create harmony or peace in East Asia.

I was born in Manchuria under Japanese rule, lived in Seoul before the Korean War, and went to Vietnam War before immigrating to the United States. I know what war means to people. This is why I am thankful to live in peace.

I am fortunate to meet Dr. Kim, who took a critical role in making this book. Also, it would not be possible to publish this book without the two professors, Kayo Nonaka and Jiayi Xu, who committed their precious time and energy to this great work.

May the Lord add His blessing to those of you.

Elder Thomas Kang
Arcola United Methodist Church

Preface

The Language Triathlon for Peacemakers of the Levine Language Center is designed to meet the needs of parallel learning of the Chinese, Japanese, and Korean languages. As you may know, the Language Triathlon project intends to use the idea that Chinese, Japanese, and Korean are similar in terms of vocabulary and grammar. Japanese uses kanji, the Chinese characters, and about 70% of Korean vocabulary also reflects Chinese character usage. Korean and Japanese also share similar grammatical structure.

This work is distinctive in that it is possible to acquire "knowledge of the differences" through simultaneous learning of the three East Asian languages. When it comes to learning three languages at the same time, readers may wonder whether it is possible and effective. (Of course, one can learn either one or two, depending on the language background of the reader.) I believe that this work can reduce such confusion by focusing on the similarities and differences between the languages. That is:

1. By comparing how common Bible verses are expressed in each language

2. By introducing how grammar is used in the other languages, you can have "knowledge of the differences." This work, however, is

not free from shortcomings. The authors feel that the work calls for updates in the future to offer better learning opportunities.

Each lesson consists of a Bible verse, new words and expressions, grammar patterns, example sentences, exercises, and activities. This text presupposes familiarity with the writing systems. Mastery of Chinese pinyin, Japanese hiragana and katakana, and Korean hangul, is recommended as early as possible. If you need information about the writing systems, basic pronunciation and available online courses with this volume, don't hesitate to get in touch with us at trilangthlon@gmail.com.

Three NYU professors have worked together to write this book over the past three years. They are Jiayi Xu, Kayo Nonaka, and Dongmin Kim. On behalf of the authors, I wish to express my appreciation to Elder Kang who never stops his encouragement, and Yong-ho Kim, CEO of Nachimvan press for the editorial tasks.

Dongmin Kim, PhD
Department of East Asian Studies, New York University

01

Matthew/마태복음/马太福音/マタイの福音書
5:9

Blessed are the peacemakers,
for they will be called children of God.

화평하게 하는 사람은 복이 있다.
그들이 하나님의 아들이라고 불릴 것이다.

使人和睦的人有福了！ 因为他们必称为神的儿子。
shǐ rén hémùde rén yǒufúle yīnwèi tāmen bì chēngwéi shénde érzi.

平和(へいわ)をつくり出す(だす)人(ひと)たちは、さいわいである、彼(かれ)らは神(かみ)の子(こ)と呼(よ)ばれるであろうれるであろう。

Chinese

使: to make, させる, ~하게 하다

人: person, 人 [ひと], 사람

和睦: harmony, 平和 [へいわ], 화평

福: blessing, さいわい, 복

因为: because, なぜなら, 왜냐하면

他们: they, 彼ら [かれら], 그들

神: God, 神 [かみ], 하나님

儿子: child, 子[こ], 아들

必: definitely, かならず [必ず], 반드시

称为: to be called (as), 呼ばれる [よばれる], 불리다

Japanese

平和: peace, 和平 [hépíng], 평화

つくる: to create, 造 [zào], 만들다

出す: to come out, 出 [chū], 내다

人: person, 人 [rén], 사람

さいわい: blessing, 福 [fú], 복

である: to be, 是 [shì], 이다

彼ら: they, 他们 [tāmen], 그들

神: God, 神 [shén], 하나님

子: child, 儿子 [érzi], 아들

と: quotation marker, 인용조사

呼ばれる: to be called, 称为 [chēngwéi], 불리다

Korean

화평: peace, 和平 [hépíng], 平和 [へいわ]

만들다: to create, 造 [zào], つくる

사람: person, 人 [rén], 人 [もの]

복: blessing, 福 [fú], さいわい

그들: they, 他们 [tāmen], 彼ら [かれら]

하나님: God, 神 [shén], 神 [かみ]

아들: child, 儿子 [érzi], 子[こ]

불리다: to be called, 称为 [chēngwéi], 呼ばれる [よばれる]

Topic-comment construction

The most distinctive feature of East Asian languages is the topic-prominent construction. That is, a sentence can consist of two components: a topic and a comment. A topic is the main idea of the sentence, whether it be a subject, object, place, or instrument. A comment indicates a statement on the topic.

In Chinese, the topic comes first and is immediately followed by the comment without particles. Japanese and Korean both use particles following the topic. The Japanese (は) and Korean (은/는) topic particles are attached behind the topic. Of the two Korean particles, '은' is used for nouns ending in consonants. Conversely, '는' is attached to nouns that end in vowels. .

Even though linguists commonly categorize Chinese as a SVO language, which is opposite to the SOV structure of Korean and Japanese, the Chinese SVO structure can also be interpreted as a topic-comment structure.

Examples

1. My older brother lives in Korea and I live in America. _ Subject

K 형은 한국에 살고 저는 미국에 살아요.

C 我哥哥住在韩国，我住在美国。

J 兄(あに)は韓国(かんこく)に住(す)んでいて、私(わたし)はアメリカに住(す)んでいます。

2. I ate. _ Object

K 밥은 먹었어요.

C 饭吃完了。(the subject "I" is omitted here because it's implied. In this case 饭 is the topic, and 吃完了 is the comment.)

J ご飯(ごはん)を食(た)べました。

3. It takes an hour by train. _ Instrument

K 기차는 한 시간 걸려요.

C 坐火车要花一个小时。

J 列車(れっしゃ)で1時間(じかん)かかります。

Possession

有; ~あり/います; ~이/가 있다: to have

有; ~あり/います; ~이/가 있다 is used to refer to possession of a person, thing, or idea.

没有/ありません /いません ~ 이/가 없다 is the opposite. When used as 'to have/to not have', 있다/없다 are usually preceded by [N이/가] in Korean. In Japanese, あります is used for inanimate subjects and います for animate subjects.

Examples

1. A: 你有弟弟吗？

B: 我没有兄弟姐妹。我是独生子。

Wǒ méiyǒu xiōngdì jiěmèi. Wǒ shì dúshēngzǐ.

2. A: 兄弟(きょうだい)がいますか？

B: 兄弟(きょうだい)はいません。一人っ子(ひとりっこ)です。

3. A: 동생이 있어요?

B: 저는 형제자매가 없어요. 외동아들이에요.

Making affirmative-negative questions

吗，か is used for Chinese and Japanese (with a rising intonation) to make an affirmative-negative question. In Korean, the vocal intonation is raised at the end of the sentence without any additional grammatical structures.

Exercise

Make questions and answers using the given conversation pair and the vocabulary list below.

1. A: 你有________吗？

B: 有/没有。

2. A: ________があり/いますか？

B: はい、あります。/いいえ、ありません。

3. A: ________이/가 있어요?

B: 예, 있어요. / 아니요, 없어요.

Vocabulary List

哥哥	오빠	あに にい 兄 / お兄さん	Older brother
弟弟	남동생	おとうと おとうと 弟 / 弟さん	Younger brother
姐姐	누나	あね ねえ 姉 / お姉さん	Older sister
妹妹	여동생	いもうと いもうと 妹 / 妹さん	Younger sister
男朋友	남자친구	かれ 彼	Boyfriend
女朋友	여자친구	かのじょ 彼女	Girlfriend
工作	일	しごと 仕事	Work, job
钱 / 现金	돈 / 현금	かね げんきん お金 / 現金	Money, cash
水	물	みず 水	water
笔	펜	ペン	pen
筷子	젓가락	はし 箸	chopsticks
位子	좌석	せき いす 席 (seat)/ 椅子 (chair)	seats

Create questions and answers about the hotel and/or hotel room you booked.

Examples

Guest: What amenity does your hotel have?

Receptionist: We have a swimming pool, a restaurant, and a gym.

A: 酒店有____________________吗？

B: 有/没有。

A: ホテルに____________________がありますか？

B: はい、あります。/いいえ、ありません。

A: 호텔에 ____________________이/가 있어요?

B: 예, 있어요. / 아니요, 없어요.

Vocabulary List

游泳池 Yóuyǒngchí	プール	수영장	pool
餐厅 Cāntīng	レストラン	식당	restaurant
酒吧 Jiǔbā	バー	바	bar
健身房 Jiànshēnfáng	フィットネスセンター	체육관	gym
早饭 Zǎofàn	朝 (あさ) ご飯 (はん)	아침식사	breakfast
冰箱 Bīngxiāng	冷蔵庫 (れいぞうこ)	냉장고	fridge
微波炉 Wéibōlú	電子 (でんし) レンジ	전자레인지	microwave
无线网络 Wúxiàn wǎngluò	ワイファイ	와이파이	wifi

02

Matthew/마태복음/马太福音/マタイの福音書
5:48

Be perfect, therefore, as your heavenly Father is perfect.

그러므로 하늘에 계신 너희 아버지가 완전하신 것처럼 너희도 완전하도록 하여라.

所以，你们要完全，　像你们的天父完全一样。
suǒyǐ,　nǐmen yào wánquán,　xiàng nǐmen de tiān fù wánquán yīyàng.

それだから、あなたがたの天(てん)の父(ちち)が完全(かんぜん)であられるように、あなたがたも 完全(かんぜん)な者(もの)となりなさい。

Common Words

therefore: 所以, それだから, 그러므로

heavenly father: 天父, 天の父, 하늘(에 계신) 아버지

to be perfect (in Chinese 完全 means 'complete'): 完全, 完全, 완전하다

like, as: 像~一样, ように, 처럼

you (plural): 你们, あなたがた, 너희

Chinese

要: should, べき, 해야 하다

Japanese

の: of, 的[・de], 의

である: to be, 是 이다

なる: to become, 成为 되다

Korean

계시다: to be (an honorific form of 있다), おられる

Subject particle

The Japanese particle が and the Korean 이/가 signify the subject behind nouns. In Japanese and Korean, a predicate comes at the end of the sentence. Unlike Japanese and Korean, Chinese language does not have a subject particle. Grammatical relationships are usually shown by either word order (Subject-Verb-Object) or independent particles in Chinese. In Chinese, when an adjective is used to state the subject, "很" (lit. very) is used in between the subject and adjective even when the degree is not strong.

■ Examples

1. 天气很好。天上没有乌云。
今日は晴れました。空には雲がありません。
날씨가 맑아요. 하늘에 구름이 없어요.

2. 我的老师很好。
私の先生はいい先生です。
제 선생님이 좋아요.

Command sentence

请+V Or V一V; ~なさい; ~아라/어라

Command sentences may have different degrees of force, including a request, demand, warning, plea, or order. The forms depend on the context of the command.

There is no specific command form in Chinese. The simplest construction is made by stating the intended command verb with the polite verb 请， such as 请坐(please sit down). However, phrases with 请 are considered formal commands, and are not commonly used in day-to-day life. Rather, verbs are often followed by 一下 to soften the tone when giving the command, e.g. "V一下"--- "看一下", though this structure sometimes also carries a sense of "having a try".

Examples

看一下！	見なさい	보아라	Have a look!
吃一下！	食べなさい	먹어라	Eat it! Take a bite.
写一下！	書きなさい	써라	Write down! Try writing it.
喝一下！	飲みなさい	마셔라	Drink it! Take a sip.

Japanese and Korean command forms, ~なさい and ~아라/어라

are used by superiors to those inferior in status, e.g. teachers to students and parents to children. For commands to a superior, request forms such as ~ください and ~어/아 주세요 are used.

Request

Strongest tone	Mild tone (suggestion)	Soft tone (formal)	Soft tone (casual) Is it okay if...
等我！ 기다려 !	等我吧！ 기다려 줘 .	请等一下！ 기다려 주세요 .	可以等我一下吗？ 기다려 줄 수 있어요 ?
给我打电话！ 전화해 !	给我打电话吧！ 전화해 줘 .	请给我打电话！ 전화해 주세요 .	可以给我打电话吗？ 전화해 줄 수 있어요 ?
教我！ 가르쳐 줘 !	教我吧！ 가르쳐 줘 !	请教我！ 가르쳐 주세요 .	可以教我吗？ 가르쳐 줄 수 있어요 ?
给我拍照！ 사진 찍어 !	给我拍照吧！ 사진 찍어 줘 .	请给我拍照！ 사진 찍어 주세요 .	可以给我拍照吗？ 사진 찍어 줄 수 있어요 ?

For request

1. Office situation

Colleague 1: Could you tell me the schedule for tomorrow?

C 请告诉我明天的时间表。

J すみません。明日のスケジュールを教えてください。

K 내일 스케줄 좀 알려 주실 수 있으세요?

Colleague 2: Just a second. I am busy right now.

I will talk to everyone later.

C 等一下。我现在很忙，我一会告诉大家。

J ちょっと待ってください。今、忙しいですから、後で皆に話します。

K 잠시만요. 지금 바쁘니까 이따가 모두에게 알려드릴게요.

Colleague 1: I see. Thank you.

C 知道了。谢谢。

J わかりました。ありがとうございます。

K 알겠습니다. 감사합니다.

Manager: Would you write a report for the meeting?

C 你会为会议写一份报告吗？

J 会議のレポートを書いてください。

K 회의 리포트를 좀 써 줄래요?

Office worker: Certainly. When do you need it?

C 当然。你什么时候需要它？

J わかりました。いつまでにしましょうか。

K 물론이죠. 언제까지 필요하세요?

Manager: Can you do it by tomorrow?

C 明天你能做到吗？

J 明日までにしできますか。

K 내일까지 할 수 있겠어요?

Office worker: Okay.

C 好的。

J わかりました。

K 그럼요.

2. Classroom situation

Teacher: Everyone, please take a look at your book.

C 请大家看一下书。

J 本を見てください。

K 여러분, 책을 봐 주세요.

Student: Okay. Teacher, can you write this character?

C 好。老师，你写一下这个字,

J はい。先生、この字を書いてください。

K 네. 선생님, 이 글자를 좀 써 주세요.

Teacher: No problem. Please wait a second.

C 没问题，等一下。

J いいですよ。ちょっと待ってください。

K 네, 잠깐 기다리세요.

Student A: I didn't bring my book today.

Can you let me take a look at your book?

C 我今天没带书。你可以给我看一下书吗？

J 今日、本を持ってこなかった。Bさんの本を見せて。

K 오늘 책을 안 가져 왔어요. 저한테 책을 좀 주실 수 있으세요?

Student B: Give me one second. I am reading it now.

C 可以等一下吗？我正在看。

J ちょっと待って。今、読んでいるから。

K 잠깐만 기다려 주세요. 지금 읽고 있어요.

Student A: Do you know how to write this character? Can you teach me?

C 这个字你会写吗？你可以教我吗？

J この漢字の書き方知ってる。教えて。

K 이 글자를 어떻게 쓰는 지 알아? 가르쳐 줄 수 있어?

Student B: Sure. Give me a pen and a piece of paper. Let's write it together.

C 好的，给我一一支笔，一张纸，我们一起写吧。

J いいよ。ペンと紙がある。一緒に書こう。

K 그럼. 연필과 종이를 줘. 같이 써 보자.

*** As you can see from the examples above, Chinese frequently utilizes "可以"(can you...) and "V一下"(lit. Do the action briefly) when making a request or command in a polite manner. Status does not affect the command form in Chinese, unlike Korean or Japanese.

3. Family

Son: Mom, I have an appointment with my friend today. Please give me a ride.

J 友達と約束があるんだけど車で送って。

C 妈妈，我今天和朋友约会。请载我一程。

K 엄마, 오늘 친구하고 약속이 있어. 차로 좀 태워 줘.

Mom: Okay, let me know what time it is.

J わかった。何時。是的。好的。

C 让我知道你的约会时间。

K 응. 알았어. 약속이 몇 시인지 알려줘.

Son: It's three PM.

J 三時。

C 下午三点。

K 오후 세 시.

4. At a restaurant

Waiter: Welcome. Have a sit here.

C 欢迎，请坐。

J いらっしゃいませ。こちらへどうぞ。

K 어서 오세요. 여기 앉으세요.

Customer: Ceasar salad and a cup of coffee, please.

C 凯撒沙拉喝一杯咖啡，谢谢。

J シーザーサラダとコーヒーをお願いします。

K 시저 샐러드하고 커피 한 잔 주세요.

Waiter: Please wait a moment.

C 请稍等。

J 少々お待ちください。

K 잠시만 기다려 주세요.

Activity 1

Have a conversation that includes a command with your classmates.

1. A is visiting a place and would like to ask B to take a picture:

2. You couldn't reach your friend by phone, so you ask him/her to call you back.

3. You are inviting your friend to come to your party.

4. You'd like your classmate to teach you language, but he/she doesn't seem to want to do so. Therefore, you'd like to politely ask them again.

5. Your colleague is leaving the office, and you'd like to go with him/her. However, you are still packing your stuff, so you ask him/her to wait for you.

Activity 2

A needs to act out the following actions while saying the following phrases:

Tell your friend to eat:

Tell your students to write:

Tell your customer to look:

Tell your child to eat (if he doesn't want to eat and you are angry with him):

Please wait for me.

Can you take a picture?

Will you marry me?

Call me tomorrow.

May I speak to John?

Could you come to my party?

Please teach me English.

Please read for me.

Please help me.

Please wait for me.

Please tell me your phone number.

Please say that again one more time.

Please speak slowly.

Activity 3

Give your directions to your new babysitter/hairdresser/waiter.

03

Matthew/마태복음/马太福音/マタイの福音書
6:33

But seek first his kingdom and his righteousness, and all these things will be given to you as well.

먼저 아버지의 나라와 아버지의 의를 구하여라.
그러면 이 모든 것들이 너희에게 덤으로 주어질 것이다.

你们要先求他的国和他的义， 这些东西都要加给你们了。
nǐmen yào xiān qiú tā de guó hé tā de yì, zhèxiē dōngxī dū yào jiā gěi nǐmenle.

まず神(かみ)の国(くに)と神(かみ)の義(ぎ)とを求(もと)めなさい。そうすれば、これらのものは、すべて添(そ)えて与え(あた)えられるであろう。

Chinese

先: first, まず, 먼저

国: kingdom/country, 国 [くに], 나라

义: righteousness, 義 [き], 의

求: to seek, もとめる [求める], 구하다

都: all, すべて, 모든

加: to add, くわえる [加える], 더하다

V.+给sb: sb. Is the receiver of the action

些: plural marker, ら, 들

这些: these, これら, 이것들

Japanese

まず: first, 先 [xiān], 먼저

神: God, 神 [shén], 하나님

国: kingdom/country, 国 [guó], 나라

義: righteousness, 义 [yì], 의

求める: to seek, 求 [qiú], 구하다

そうすれば: if so, 那样一来 [nàyàng yīlái], 그렇게 하면

これら: these, 这些 [zhèxiē], 이것들

もの: thing/person, ~的, 것

すべて: all, 都 [dōu], 모두

添える: to add, 添 [tiān], 더하다

与える: to give, 与 [yǔ], 주다

Korean

먼저: first, 先 [xiān], まず

아버지: father, 父 [fù], ちち [父]

나라: kingdom/country, 国 [guó], 国 [くに]

의: righteousness, 义 [yì], 義 [き]

구하다: to seek, 求 [qiú], もとめる [求める]

그러면: if so, 那样一来 [nàyàng yīlái], そうすれば

이: this, 这 [zhè], これ

모든: all, 都, すべて

덤: an addition, 饶头[ráo · tou], けいひん [景品]

주어지다: to be given

Conjunction for addition

和，と，and 와/과 are phrasal conjunctions that connect nouns or noun phrases in lists. There are separate conjunctions for connecting clauses, which will be discussed later. 和，と，and 와/과 can also be used as prepositions. In Japanese, と is commonly used to mean いっしょに。In Korean, the 와/과 construction can substitute for 함께 or 같이 meaning "together".

Examples

C 我和她都喜欢喝茶。Both she and I like drinking tea.

我喜欢和她一起喝茶。I like drinking tea with her.

J 僕と彼女はお茶を飲むことが好きだ。

私は彼女とお茶を飲むことが好きだ。

K 나와 그녀는 차를 마시는 것을 좋아해요.

나는 그녀와 차를 마시는 것을 좋아해요.

Exercise

1. Make list what is your favorite Asian foods using the conjunctions.

C 我喜欢__________和__________。

J 私は __________ と ____________________が好きです。

K 저는 __________ 와/과 ____________________를 좋아해요.

C 早饭我常常吃________和__________。For breakfast, I usually eat________and________.

午饭我常常吃________和__________。For lunch, I usually eat________and________.

晚饭我常常吃________和_________。For dinner, I usually eat ________ and ________.

J 朝(あさ)ごはんに________と__________を食(た)べます。

昼(ひる)ごはんに________と__________を食(た)べます。

晩(ばん)ごはんに________と__________を食(た)べます。

K 아침 식사로 ___________와/과 ___________를 주로 먹어요.

점심 식사로 ___________와/과 ___________를 주로 먹어요.

저녁 식사로 ___________와/과 ___________를 주로 먹어요.

2. Ask each other what they like to do with friends and family.

C A: 你喜欢和家人一起做什么？

B: 我喜欢和家人一起 ___________。

A: 你喜欢和朋友一起做什么？

B: 我喜欢和朋友一起 ___________。

J A: 家族(かぞく)といっしょに何(なに)をしますか。

B: ___________。

A: 友達(ともだち)といっしょに何(なに)をしますか。

B: ___________。

K A: 가족과 같이 주로 뭐 하는 거 좋아하세요?

B: ___________.

A: 친구와 같이 주로 뭐 하는 거 좋아하세요?

B: ___________.

Vocabulary List

喜欢 like	好(す)き	좋아하다
常常 often, usually	たいてい	주로
早饭 breakfast	朝(あさ)ごはん	아침 식사
午饭 lunch	昼(ひる)ごはん	점심 식사
晚饭 dinner	晩(ばん)ごはん	저녁 식사
家人 family	家族(かぞく)	가족
朋友 friends	友達(ともだち)	친구
一起 together	いっしょに	같이 / 함께
做 do	する・します	하다
吃饭 eat	食(た)べる・食(た)べます	밥을 먹다

喝茶 drink tea	お茶(ちゃ)を飲(の)む・飲(の)みます	차를 마시다
喝咖啡 drink coffee	コーヒーを飲(の)む・飲(の)みます	커피를 마시다
旅行 travel	旅行(りょこう)する・旅行(りょこう)します	여행하다
打游戏 play games	ゲームをする・します	게임하다
买东西 shopping	買(か)い物(もの)する・(か)い物(もの)します	쇼핑하다
去教会 go to the church	教会(きょうかい)へ行(い)く・行(い)きます	교회에 가다

Demonstratives

Demonstratives indicate the physical or mental proximity of an item relative to the speaker and the listener. In Chinese, demonstratives are usually followed by a measure word/counter. The most common measure word is 个.

这	この (+N), これ	이	this
那	その (+N), それ	그	that (close to listener)
	あの (+N), あれ	저	that over there
哪	どの (+N), どれ	어느	which, a certain
这些			These
那些			Those
哪些			Which ones

A: How much is this loaf of bread?

B: Which one? Ah, that one is $1.

A: How much is that cake over there?

B: That one over there is $12.

C A: 这个面包多少钱？

B: 哪个面包？啊~那个面包1美元。

A: 那个蛋糕多少钱？

B: 那个蛋糕十二美元。

J A: このパンはいくらですか？

B: どれですか？そのパンは1ドルです。

A: あのケーキは？

B: あのケーキは12ドルです。

K A: 이 빵은 얼마예요?

B: 어느 빵이요? 아 ~ 그 빵은 1불이에요.

A: 저 케익은요?

B: 저 케익은 12불이에요.

Activity

Make a conversation by pointing at things in your place.

04

Matthew/마태복음/马太福音/マタイの福音書
16:16

Simon Peter answered, “You are the Messiah, the Son of the living God.”

시몬 베드로가 대답하였습니다.
“주님은 그리스도이시며, 살아계신 하나님의 아들이십니다.”

西门·彼得回答说： 你是基督，是永生 神的儿子。
Xīmén·bǐdé huídá shuō: Nǐ shì jīdū, shì yǒngshēng shén de érzi.

シモン・ペテロが答（こた）えて答(こた)えた、「あなたこそ、生(い)ける神(かみ)の子(こ)キリストです」。

Common Words

西门·彼得, シモン・ペテロ, 시몬 베드로: Simon Peter

回答, 答える, 대답하다: to answer

基督, キリスト, 그리스도: Christ, Messiah

儿子, 子, 아들: son

Chinese

说: to speak, とく [説く], 말하다

是: to be, です, 이다

永生: eternal life, えいせい [永生], 영생

Japanese

-こそ: polite/intimate particle after a person's name or pronoun

生ける: to live, 活 [huó], 살아있다

Korean

주님: Lord, 主 [zhǔ], しゅ [主]

살아계시다: to live (honorific form of 살아있다), 活 [huó], いける [生ける]

Copula "to be": 是，です，~이다

In the topic-comment structure, the copula is located before the second noun in Chinese and behind the second noun in Japanese and Korean in order to complete the comment. The conjugation for Korean "~이다" is realized as "~이에요" for a noun ending in a consonant and "~예요" for a consonant ending in a vowel in polite speech. The topic comment structure is also a distinctive linguistic feature of Chinese language, and is created using 是 following the subject. It is also acceptable to omit 是 in the sentence, especially in spoken language, e.g. 我厨师，他中国人。

我是厨师。我妻子是老师。
私はシェフです。妻は、先生です。
저는 요리사예요. 제 아내는 선생님이에요.
I am a cook. My wife is a teacher.

Exercise

Take a guess at your partner's nationality and occupation.

A: Are you Japanese?
B: Yes, I am Japanese.

A: 你是日本人吗？

B: 是，我是日本人。

A: Are you a teacher?

B: No, I am a computer engineer.

A: 你是老师吗？

B: 不是，我是电脑工程师。

Past tense

Chinese does not have any verb conjugations to indicate tense and speech style. All verbs have a single form. For example, the verb for "eat" is 吃 (chī), which can be used for the past, present, and future. Despite the lack of verb conjugations, there are ways to express time frames in Chinese, such as time adverbs.

In Japanese, the conjugation patterns vary depending on the speech style as shown below.

Verbs：stem + ます/ませんでした

食べました　食べませんでした (polite speech style)

食べた　食べなかった (casual speech style)

I-adjectives: take out the last syllable い and put かった/かったです。

おいしかったです　おいしくなかったです (polite speech style)

おいしかった　おいしくなかった (casual speech style)

Na-adjectives: add でした/じゃなかったです

げんきでした　げんきじゃなかったです (polite speech style)

げんきだった　げんきじゃなかった (casual speech style)

Copula:

でした　じゃなかったです (polite speech style)

だった　じゃなかった (casual speech style)

In Korean, ~었/았/ㅆ indicates that the event described has already taken place. ~았 is used for verbs/adjectives with a consonant ending that have "ㅏ" or "ㅗ" in the final syllable of the stem, (eg., 받았어요, (I) received). ~었 is used for verbs/adjectives with final vowels other than "ㅏ" or "ㅗ" (eg., 먹었어요, (I) ate). "ㅆ" is used for the verbs/adjectives that end in a vowel (eg., 갔어요, (I) went). In addition, verb/adjective predicates that end in "~하다" are conjugated as "~했다" (eg., 공부했어요, (I) studied).

A: What did you do yesterday?

B: I watched TV.

C A: 你昨天做了什么？

B: 我昨天看了电视。

J A: 昨日何をしましたか？

B: (私は)テレビを見ました。

K A: 어제 뭐 했어요?

B: 텔레비전을 봤어요.

Exercise

Answer the questions in each language using the appropriate tense.

1. A: What did you eat for dinner yesterday?

B: ______________________________.

2. A: Where were you last Sunday?

B: ______________________________.

3. A: Who did you meet last weekend?

B: ______________________________.

4. A: What did you receive for your birthday?

B: ______________________________.

5. A: What time did you get up this morning?

B: ______________________________.

05

Mark/마가복음/马可福音/マルコの福音書
10:45

For even the Son of Man did not come to be served, but to serve, and to give his life as a ransom for many.

인자도 섬김을 받으려고 온 것이 아니라, 섬기려고 왔다. 인자는 자기 생명을 많은 사람의 대속물로 주려고 왔다.

因为人子来，并不是要受人的服事，　　乃是要服事人，
yīn wéi rén zǐ lái, bìng bùshì yào shòu rén de fú shì, nǎi shì yào fú shì rén,
并且要舍命作多人的 赎价。
bìngqiě yào shěmìng zuò duō rén de shú jià.

人(ひと)の子(こ)がきたのも、仕(つか)えられるためではなく、使(つか)えるためであり、また多(おお)くの人(ひと)のあがないとして、自分(じぶん)の命(いのち)を与える(あた)えるためである。

Common Words

人子, 人の子 [ひとのこ], 인자: the Son of Man

来, くる [来る], 오다: to come

服事, つかえる [仕える], 섬기다: to serve

赎价, あがない, 속죄/대속물: ransom

多, おおく [多く], 많다: to be many

不是~乃是, ~ためではなく, ~이/가 아니라: not for ~ but

Chinese

因为: because, なぜなら, 왜냐하면

不是, 乃…: not only…, but also : ~만 아니라, 하지만 또한

受: to receive, 受ける [うける], 받다

并且: and, そして, 그리고

舍: to abandon, すてる [捨てる], 버리다

命: life, いのち [命], 생명

Japanese

ためである: to be due to, 由于 [yóuyú], 때문이다

また: also, 也 [yě], 또한

与える: to give, 给与 [gěiyǔ], 주다

Korean

섬김: service, 服事 [fúshì], つかえ [仕え]

받다: to receive, 受 [shòu], 受ける [うける]

자기: self, 己 [jǐ], じしん [自身]

생명: life, 命 [mìng], いのち [命]

주다: to give, 给与 [gěiyǔ], 与える[あたえる]

Negative equational expressions: A is not B

不是，ではない/じゃないです，~이/가 아니다

C For the negation of the copula,

you can simply put the negative marker 不 before 是 in Chinese. Note that in Chinese, the negation marker 不 is an adverb, and therefore should be placed before verb 是。

J ではない is the negative form of the copula である in Japanese. The regular conversational form is じゃないです, which is the negative of です (as in Lesson 4).

K For Korean, you attach 이/가 to the second noun and then use 아니다. The conjugation for Korean is realized as "~이 아니에요" for nouns ending in consonants and "~가 아니에요" for nouns ending in vowels in polite speech.

Examples

A：Is your mother also a teacher?

C 你妈妈也是老师吗？

J 兄お母さんは先生ですか。

K 어머니도 선생님이에요?

B：No, my mother is not a teacher.

C 不是，我妈妈不是老师。

J いいえ、先生じゃありません。

K 아니요, 선생님이 아니에요.

A: Are you a Canadian?

C 你是加拿大人吗？

J カナダ人ですか。

K 캐나다 사람이에요?

B: No, I am not a Canadian. I am an American.

C 我不是加拿大人，我是美国人。

J いいえ、カナダ人じゃありません。アメリカ人です。

K 아니요, 캐나다 사람이 아니에요. 미국 사람이에요.

Exercise

Fill in the blanks to complete the conversation.

A: 这是寿司吗？これはすしですか。

이거 스시예요? Is this sushi?

B: 是寿司。はい、すしです。

네, ______________. Yes, it is sushi.

A: 那也是寿司吗？あれもすしですか。저것도 스시예요?

Is that sushi too?

B: 不是，是紫菜包饭。いいえ、あれはキンパです。

아니요, ______________. 김밥이에요.

No, ______________. It's kimbab.

A: 这是意大利面吗？これはスパゲティーですか。

이거 스파게티예요? Is this spaghetti?

B: 是意大利面。はい、スパゲティーです。

네, ________________. Yes, ______________.

A: 那也是意大利面吗？あれもスパゲティーですか。

저것도 스파게티예요? Is that spaghetti too?

B: 不是，是炒面。いいえ、あれはスパゲティーじゃありません。

焼きそばです。아니요, ______________. 볶음면이에요.

No, it is not spaghetti. It is fried noodles.

A: 碧昂丝是西班牙人吗？ビヨンセはスペイン人ですか。

비욘세는 스페인 사람이에요? Is Beyonce Spanish?

B: 她不是西班牙人，是美国人。いいえ、スペイン人ではありません。アメリカ人です。

아니요, ______________________. 미국 사람이에요.

No, she is not Spanish. She is an American.

A: 艾玛。沃特森是美国人吗？エマ・ワトソンはアメリカ人ですか。엠마 왓슨은 미국 사람이에요?

Is Emma Watson an American?

B: 不是，她是英国人。いいえ、アメリカ人じゃありません。イギリス人です。아니요, ________________. 영국 사람이에요.

No, she is not. She is British.

Purpose or intention

要/为了/(是为了) ために/に，~려고: (in order) to

C The Chinese auxiliary verb 要 has several meanings such as "want to do", "need to do" and "be going to do". It can also be followed by a noun, which means "want something". 想 is sometimes interchangeable with 要，but it has a meaning closer to "would like to do". "为了/是为了" is the most commonly used phrase to indicate one's purpose or intention.

J The Japanese connective suffix ために indicates the purpose in general, while verb stem + に is used with motion verbs such as to go, to come, to return etc.. Both ために and に can be used with nouns such as 仕事のために/仕事に。ために also indicates a reason or cause. ～ためです can also be used.

K The Korean connective suffix ~려고 does not necessarily

involve motion verbs as in Japanese, and instead attaches to "purpose" verbs. This suffix follows up action verbs in order to describe the purpose of the action.

Examples

He came (here) in order to serve people.

C 他来要服事人们。

J 彼は人々に仕えるために来た。

K 그는 사람들을 섬기려고 왔어요.

(I) am studying hard in order to get a scholarship.

C 我努力学习是为了获得奖学金。

J 奨学金をもらうために熱心に勉強しています。

K 장학금을 받으려고 열심히 공부해요.

(I) went to Europe for a trip.

C 我去欧洲是为了去旅行。

J ヨーロッパへ旅行に行きました。

K 유럽에 여행하려고 갔어요.

(I) bought a dictionary for Kanji study (studying Kanji).

C 我买了一本字典是为了学习汉字。

J 漢字の勉強のために辞書を書いました。

K 한자를 공부하려고 사전을 샀어요.

This dictionary is for studying Kanji.

C 这是一本学汉字的字典。

J この辞書は漢字の勉強のためです。

K 이 사전은 한자를 공부하려는 것이에요.

(I) will go to the cafe to drink coffee.

C 我要去餐厅喝咖啡。

J コーヒーを飲みにカフェへ行きます。

K 커피를 마시려고 해요.

(I) will go home to eat dinner.

C 我要回家吃晚饭。

J 晩ごはんを食べにうちへ帰ります。

K 저녁을 먹으려고 해요.

Exercise

1. Fill in the blanks to complete the conversation.

C A: 你为什么要去韩国

B: 我为了 ____________ (+purpose) 去韩国学习韩语。

J A: なぜ韓国に行きますか？

B: 韓国語を ____________ 韓国に行きます。

K A: 왜 한국에 가세요?

B: 한국어를 ____________ 한국에 가요.

2. Complete the table and make a conversation with the contents.

C A: 你为什么要省钱？

J 何のためにお金を貯めていますか？

K 왜 저축하세요? (what you are doing)

C 我要省钱是为了买房子。

K 집을 사려고 저축해요.

J 家を買うために貯金しています。(purpose)

Purpose	What you are doing
	省钱 貯金する 저축하다
要幸福 幸せになる 행복해지다	

	学习外语 外国語を学ぶ 외국어를 배우다
找工作 就職する 취직하다	

1) 你要做什么？/ 何をしに行きますか。/ 뭐(를) 할 거예요? /
What are you going to do?
图书馆 / 図書館 / 도서관/ library
学校 / 学校 / 학교 / school
餐厅 / レストラン / 식당 / restaurant
超级 / ーパー / 수퍼 / supermarket

2) I am studying to become a lawyer.
why, what for~ / 为什么 / どうして/何のために～ / 왜, 뭐 때문에~ /
C 我要学习是为了成为一名律师。
J 弁護士になるために勉強しています。
K 변호사가 되려고 공부해요.

3) I am working to buy a car.
C 我打工是为了买车。
J 車を買うためにアルバイトをしています。
K 차를 사려고 아르바이트를 해요.

4) I am learning Japanese culture because I want to study abroad in Japan.

C 我学日本文化是为了去日本留学。

J 日本を文化を学ぶために日本へ留学します。

K 일본 문화를 배우려고 일본에 유학해요.

5) I practice hard to do well.

C 我努力练习是为了做得更好。

J 上手になるために一生懸命練習します。

K 잘 하려고 열심히 연습해요.

06

Luke/누가복음/路加福音/ルカの福音書
12:15

Then he said to them, “Watch out! Be on your guard against all kinds of greed; life does not consist in an abundance of possessions.”

그리고 사람들에게 말씀하셨다. “너희는 조심하여, 온갖 탐욕을 멀리하여라. 재산이 차고 넘치더라도, 사람의 생명은 거기에 달려 있지 않다.”

于是对众人说：　「你们要谨慎自守，　去一切的贪心，
Yúshì duì zhòngrén shuō: `Nǐmen yào jǐnshèn zì shǒu, miǎn qù yīqiè de tānxīn,
因为人的生命 不在乎家道丰富。
yīn wéi rén de shēngmìng bùzàihū jiā dào fēngfù.

それから人々(ひとびと)にむかって言(い)われた、「あらゆる貪欲(どんよく)に対(たい)してよくよく警戒(けいかい)しなさい。たといたくさんの物(もの)を持(も)っていても、人(ひと)のいのちは、持(も)ち物(もの)にはよらないのである」。

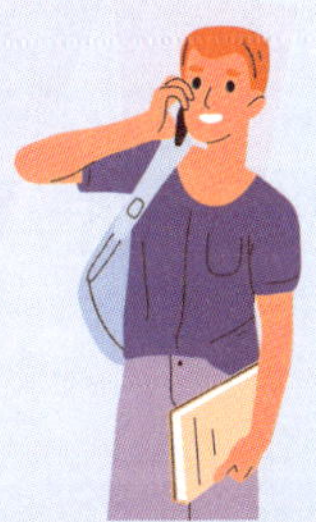

Common Words

众人, 人々 [ひとびと], 사람들: people

说, とく [説く], 말하다: to speak

谨慎, ちゅういする [注意する], 경계하다: cautious, to guard against

免去, はずす [外す], 없애다: to remove

一切, あらゆる, 온갖: all

贪心, 貪欲 [どんよく], 탐욕: greed

因为, なぜなら, 왜냐하면: because

生命, いのち, 생명: life

家道丰富, 財産 [ざいさん], 재산: possessions

Chinese

于是: then, 続けて, 이어서

自: self, 自己, 자기

守: to guard, 守る, 지키다

在乎: to care about, 気にします, 신경쓰다

Japanese

それから: and then, 然后 [ránhòu], 그리고 나서

むかう: to face, 向 [xiàng], 향하다

対して: for/in regard to, 对 [duì], 대하여

よくよく: very/exceedingly, 仔细地 [zǐxìde], 꼼꼼히

警戒: alert, 警戒 [jǐngjiè], 경계

たとい: even if, 就算 [jiùsuàn], 설령

たくさん: a lot, 多 [duō], 많음

持つ: to take, 持 [chí], 가지다

よる: to be due to, 因 [yīn], 인하다

Korean

그리고: and, 然后 [ránhòu], そうして

조심하다: to be careful, 小心 [xiǎo xīn], つつしむ [慎む]

멀리하다: to guard against, 警戒 [jǐngjiè], ちゅういする [注意する]

재산: possessions, 财产 [cáichǎn], 財産 [ざいさん]

차다: to be full, 充满 [chōngmǎn], みちる [満ちる]

넘치다: to overflow, あふれる [溢れる], 溢出 [yìchū]

달려있다: to depend on, 有赖 [yǒulài], ある [在る]

Goal/Target marker: 对，に，에게

These three affixes can be used to indicate that you are doing (usually giving) something TO somebody. Chinese 对 is prepositional whereas Japanese に and Korean 에게 are postpositional. In Chinese, 对 indicates "to" or "towards" an object or target, which the action directly performs on, occurring with intransitive verb and adjective. 给 on the other hand, when used as a verb, it means physically give someone something, occurring with transitive verb. More frequently, 给 is used as a preposition to introduce the beneficiary or the receiver of the action. It often translates to "for/for the sake of" in English.

Thomas is very nice to Jenniffer.
C 汤玛士对珍妮佛很好。
J トーマスはジェニファーに(対して)優しいです。
K 토마스가 제니퍼에게 친절해요.

Thomas said to Jennifer.
C 汤玛士对珍妮佛说。
J トーマスはジェニファーに言いました。
K 토마스가 제니퍼에게 말했어요.

Chinese is difficult for me.
C 中文对我很难。
J 中国語は私にとって難しいです。
K 중국어가 저에게 어려워요.

I'm interested in Chinese.
C 我对中文很有兴趣。

J 中国語に興味があります。

K (저는) 중국어에 관심있어요.

Japanese に is used with a noun to mean the direction of the action. に can be replaced with へ。

I go to the library.

図書館(としょかん)に行(い)きます。

I call my friend.

友達(ともだち)に電話(でんわ)をします。

に can be also used with a verb stem form with another verb such as いく、くる、かえる etc. indicating going from one point to another.

I go to the library to study.

図書館に勉強(べんきょう)しに行きます。

I go home to have lunch.

昼ごはんを食べに家に帰ります。

Korean 에게 can be replaced with 한테 that is more spoken and 께 that is for honorific. For the inanimate objects, 에 is used.

Examples

1. What did you give to your friends?

C 你给你朋友什么？

J 友達に何を上げましたか。

K 친구들한테 뭐 (를) 주었어?

2. I sent an email to my teacher yesterday.

C 我昨天给老师发了邮件。

J 昨日先生にEメールを送りました。

K (나는) 어제 선생님께 이메일을 보냈어요.

3. My mom called me in the morning.

C 我妈妈今天早上给我打了电话。

J 母は(私に)電話してきました。

K 엄마가 아침에 (저한테) 전화했어요.

(Japanese and Korean don't usually use it when it is explicit by context.)

4. Do you often call your home?

C 你常常给家里打电话吗？

J 家に電話しますか。

K 집에 자주 전화하세요?

5. I water the plants every morning.

C 我每天早上给植物浇水。

J 毎朝植木に水をやります。

K 매일 아침 화분에 물을 줘요.

Exercise

Make conversations with your classmates about what were the gifts for your friends/family last Christmas.

A: 去年圣诞节你给朋友/家人什么？

B: 我给____________。

Negation

不，ない，~지 않다: to not be

Although there are a number of negative expressions in each language, the most common one is 不 for Chinese, ない for Japanese, and ~지 않다/안, for Korean.

Japanese「ない」is plain form. The polite style is 「ません」. Verbs and adjectives conjugate a bit differently.

To drive, to not drive. 運転する、運転しない。

I will drive, I will not drive. 運転します、運転しません。

Good, bad/not good. いいです、よくないです/よくありません。

It's lively, it's not lively / it's not lively にぎやかです、にぎやかじゃないです/にぎやかじゃありません。

The Korean negative ~지 않다 is located behind a verb/adjective and 안 occurs before the verb/adjective, which is interchangeable.

The weather is not good.

I don't drive.

C 天气不好。

我不开车。

J 天気はよくない。/よくありません。(よくないです。)

私は運転しない。/運転しません。

K 날씨가 좋지 않아요. / 날씨가 안 좋아요.

저는 운전하지 않아요. / 저는 운전 안 해요.

Exercise

Make a conversation based on the following questions:

1. 什么不贵？ 何が高くないですか。뭐가 안 비싸요? What's not expensive?

2. 什么不多？ 何が多くないですか。뭐가 안 많아요? What's not many/much?

3. 什么不好吃？ 何がおいしくないですか。뭐가 안 맛있어요? What's not delicious?

4. 什么不大？ 何が大きくないですか。뭐가 안 커요? What's not big?

5. 什么不好看？ 何が뭐가 보기 안 좋아요? What's bad-looking?

6. 什么不便宜？ 何が安くないですか。뭐가 안 싸요? What's not cheap?

7. 什么不干净？ 何がきれいじゃないですか。뭐가 안 깨끗해요? What's not clean?

8. 什么不好？ 何がよくないですか。뭐가 안 좋아요? What's not good?

07

John/요한복음/约翰福音/ヨハネの福音書
1:12

Yet to all who did receive him, to those who believed in his name, he gave the right to become children of God.

그를 맞아들인 사람들, 곧 그 이름을 믿는 사람들에게는 하나님의 자녀가 되는 특권을 주셨다.

凡接待他的，就是信他名的人，
Fán jiēdài tā de, jiùshì xìn tā míng de rén,
他就赐他们权柄作神的儿女。
tā jiù cì tāmen quánbǐng zuò shénde érnǚ.

彼(かれ)を受(う)けいれけいれた者(もの)、すなわち、その名(な)を信(しん)じた人々(ひとびと)には、彼(かれ)は神(かみ)の子(こ)となる力(ちから)を与(あた)えたのである。

Common Words

接待, 受けいれる, 맞아 들이다: to receive, accept

就, すなわち, 곧: in other words, that is

信, しんじる[信じる] 믿다: to believe

名, なまえ, 이름: name

赐, 与える [あたえる], 주다: to give

权柄, 力, 힘: power

儿女, 子ども, 자녀: children

Chinese

凡: all, any, およそ [凡そ], 무릇

作: to become, なる, 되다.

Japanese

なる: to become, 成为 [chéngwéi], 되다

力: power, 力, 힘

Korean

특권: privilege, 特权 [tèquán], とっけん [特権]

Attributive construction

Chinese 的，Japanese plain form, Korean은 In general, the word order of Chinese is different from Korean and Japanese in that Chinese sentences follow SVO structure, whereas Japanese and Korean are SOV languages. However, in terms of the position of an attributive, the three languages are the same. An attributive is always placed before the noun it modifies, not after (unlike the English grammar structure).

When a noun is described or attributed by elements such as a clause, phrase, or word, the noun-modifier 的, plain form, 는 occur prior to the noun and after the modifying element. Unlike Chinese, Korean noun-modifiers vary depending on the tense. Here, 는 is used for present tense verbs. 은 is used for both past tense verbs and present tense adjectives. Japanese plain forms change depending on the tense and aspects of affirmative or negative descriptors. These changes also apply to verbs, adjectives and nouns.

Adjective/Phrase modifying a noun

- delicious meal　好吃的饭　おいしい食事　맛있는 음식
- pretty school　漂亮的学校　きれいな学校　예쁜 학교
- expensive stuff　很贵的东西　高い物　비싼 물건

- nice weather　很好的天气　いい天気　좋은 날씨
- delicious and inexpensive restaurant　好吃不贵的饭馆　おいしくて安いレストラン　맛있고 싼 식당

Attributive clause modifying a noun

- the food my mom made/makes　妈妈做的饭　母が作った/作る料理　엄마가 만드는 음식
- people who live in New York　住在纽约的人　ニューヨークに住んでいる人　뉴욕에 사는 사람들
- teacher who teaches Japanese　教日文的老师　日本語を教えている先生　일본어를 가르치는 선생님
- the guest who speaks Chinese　说中文的客人　中国語を話すお客　중국어를 하는 손님
- the character I don't recognize　我不认识的字　知らない人物　내가 모르는 사람

Here are some examples of attributive clauses in the past tense.

- the store Tanaka went to　田中さんが行った店
- the sandwich we ate yesterday　昨日食べたサンドイッチ
- the book I read at the library　図書館で読んだ本
- the restaurant whose service was bad　サービスが悪かったレストラン
- the period the study was hard (when I was having a hard time

studying　勉強が大変だった時期

- the year I was an international student.　留学生だった年

Tense is not specified in the attributive clause in Chinese, and must be interpreted based on context.

Examples

1. Someone whom I don't know called me.

C 我不认识的人给我打了一个电话。

J 知らない人が電話をしてきました。

K 내가 모르는 사람이 전화했어요.

2. The food my mom makes is very delicious.

C 我妈妈做的饭很好吃。

J 母が作る料理はとてもおいしいです。

K 엄마가 만드는 음식은 아주 맛있어요.

3. You can receive/welcome the guests who speak Chinese.

C 你可以接待说中文的客人。

J 中国語を話すお客さんを受け入れられます。

K 중국어를 말하는 손님들을 맞이할 수 있어요.

4. Many people who live in New York take the subway.

C 很多住在纽约的人坐地铁。

J ニューヨークに住む人はよく地下鉄に乗ります。

K 뉴욕에 사는 많은 사람들이 지하철을 타요.

Exercise

1. Based on the English sentence, rearrange the following words to create a sentence.

Please teach me how to write the characters I don't recognize.

C 我、我、不、写、的、请、字 教、认识

K 모르는, 가르쳐 주세요, 제가, 쓰는 지, 글자, 어떻게

Our university has many teachers who teach Japanese.

C 大学、老师、很多、日文、有、的、我们、教

K 일본어를, 선생님들이, 대학에, 가르치는, 많아요, 우리

2. (1) Please fill in the blank to describe the given noun.

Morzart is a person who…

モーツアルトは(　　　　)人です。

John Lennon is a person who…

ジョンレノンは(　　　　)人です。

Library is a place where…

図書館は(　　　　)所です。

School is a place where…

学校は(　　　　)所です。

A camera is a thing …

カメラは(　　　　)物です。

(2) Please combine the following two sentences:

The teacher wrote a kanji.

J 先生は漢字を書きました。

K 선생님께서 한자를 가르쳤어요.

C 这个老师写了一个汉字。

I don't understand the kanji.

J その漢字がわかりません。

K 저는 한자를 몰라요.

C 我不认识这个汉字。

The teacher wrote a kanji that I don't understand.

I ate the breakfast that I made this morning.

J 今朝朝ごはんを作りました。

K 오늘 아침에 아침을 만들었어요.

C 我今天早上做了早饭。

J その朝ごはんを食べました。

K 그 아침을 먹었어요.

C 我吃了早饭。

The sweater (I) bought is pretty.

J セーターを買いました。

K 스웨터를 샀어요.

C 我买了一件毛衣。

J そのセーターはきれいです。

K 그 스웨터가 예뻐요.

C 这件毛衣很好看。

3. Ask your classmates to find people who meet the description below using each of the three languages.

- Who is the person who lives in the dormitory?
- Who is the person who drives the car?
- Who is the person who is junior?
- Who is the person who swims well?

Object particle

The object of the sentence is unmarked in Chinese. When a verb takes an object, no object particle is used. This is very different from Japanese and Korean, in which を and 을/를 are used in between object and verb.

Examples

1. Lisa studies Korean.

- **C** 丽莎学韩文。
- **J** リサは韓国語を勉強しています。
- **K** 리사가 한국어를 공부해요.

2. Jenny meets her friend on Saturday.

- **C** 珍妮星期六跟她朋友见面。
- **J** ジェニーは土曜日に友達に会います。
- **K** 제니가 토요일에 친구를 만나요.

3. My dad cleans the house.

- **C** 我妈妈打扫房间。
- **J** 父は部屋を掃除します。
- **K** 아버지께서 집을 청소해요.

4. I took a taxi to go to the airport.

C 我坐出租车去机场。

J タクシーに乗って空港に行きました。

K 공항에 가려고 택시를 탔어요.

5. Take the subway.

C 坐地铁

J 地下鉄に乗ってください。

K 지하철을 타세요.

6. Teach me Korean.

C 教我韩文。

J 韓国語を教えてください。

K 한국어를 가르쳐 주세요.

7. I cook Chinese food everyday.

C 我每天做中国菜。

J 毎日中国料理を作ります。

K 매일 중국 음식을 만들어요.

8. I like learning characters. (you mean writing Chinese characters?)

C 我喜欢学汉字。

J 漢字を勉強するのが好きです。

K 한자를 공부하는 것을 좋아해요.

9. I would like to buy a cup of coffee.

C 我想买一杯咖啡。

J コーヒを買いたいです。

K 커피를 사고 싶어요.

10. Go to school.

C 去学校

J 学校へ行ってください。

K 학교에 가세요.

Exercise

Choose the appropriate verb and object combination from the table below and answer the questions.

<table>
<tr><th>Verb</th><th>Object</th></tr>
<tr><td>做 하다 to do</td><td rowspan="5">饭,음식 , food、中国菜,중국요리 , Chinese food、日本菜, 일본요리 , Japanese food、韩国菜，한국요리 , Korean Food、

衣服，옷 , clothes、蛋糕，케이크 , cake、咖啡，커피 , coffee、茶, 차 , tea、绿茶, 녹차 , green tea、红茶, 홍차 , black tea、奶茶，우유차 , milk tea、

电视，티비 , TV、电影，영화 , Film、中国电视，중국티비 , Chinese TV、韩国电视，한국티비 , Korean TV、日本电视，일본티비 , Japanese TV、美国电视，미국티비 , American TV、中国电影，중국영화 , Chinese film、韩国电影，한국영화 , Korean Film、日本电影，일본영화 , Japanese film、美国电影 , 미국영화 , American film</td></tr>
<tr><td>吃 먹다 to eat</td></tr>
<tr><td>喝 마시다 to drink</td></tr>
<tr><td>买 사다 to buy</td></tr>
<tr><td>看 보다 to watch/see</td></tr>
</table>

Question 1:

Q: What do you like to do?

C 你喜欢做什么？

J 何をしたいですか。

K 뭐 하는 거 좋아해요?

A: 我喜欢Verb+object.

Question 2:

Q: What do you usually do on weekends?

C 你周末常常做什么？

J 週末、たいてい何をしますか。

K 주말에 보통 뭐 하세요?

A: 我周末常常Verb+object.

Question 3:

Q: What do you want to do the most right now?

C 你现在最想做什么？

J 今一番何がしたいですか。

K 지금 뭘 가장 하고 싶어요?

A: 我现在最想Verb+object.

08

John/요한복음/约翰福音/ヨハネの福音書
3:16

For God so loved the world that he gave his one and only Son, that whoever believes in him shall not perish but have eternal life.

하나님이 세상을 이처럼 사랑하셔서 독생자를 주셨으니, 누구든지 그를 믿으면 멸망하지 않고 영생을 얻을 것이다.

神爱世人， 甚至将他的独生子赐给他们，
Shén ài shìrén, shènzhì jiāng tā de dúshēngzǐ cì gěi tāmen,
叫一切信他的， 不致灭亡， 反得永生。
jiào yīqiè xìn tā de, bùzhì mièwáng, fǎn dé yǒngshēng.

神(かみ)はそのひとり子(ご)を賜(たま)わったほどに、この世(よ)を愛(あい)して下(くだ)さった。それは御子(みこ)を信(しん)じる者(もの)がひとりも滅(ほろ)びないで、永遠(えいえん)の命(いのち)を得(え)るためである。

Common Words

爱, 愛 [あい]する, 사랑하다: to love

世, 世[よ], 세상: world

独生子, ひとり子, 독생자: one and only son

信: to believe, 信じる [しんじる], 믿다.

灭亡: to perish, ほろびる [滅びる], 멸망하다.

得: to have, to get 得る [える], 얻다.

永生: eternal life, えいせい [永生], 영생

Chinese

赐: to give, 与える [あたえる], (윗사람이 아랫사람에게) 주다.

叫: to make, させる, 하도록 하다.

一切: all, あらゆる, 모든

致: to arrive, 至る [いたる], 이르다.

反: rather, かえって, 도리어

Japanese

たまわる [賜(わ)る]: 주시다. (상급자로부터)

下さる: to give, 주시다. (상급자로부터)

御子 [みこ]: Son of God, 神的儿子, 하나님의 아들

永遠: everlasting, 永远 [yǒngyuǎn], 영원

Korean

이처럼: like this, 如此 [rúcǐ], こんなに

주다: to give, 赐 [cì], 与える [あたえる]

누구든지: whoever, 人人 [rénrén], だれしも [誰しも]

Korean probability : ~을 것이다

In daily life, the expression that indicates the potentiality/probability occurs frequently. There are a variety of ways to express this probability. The Korean phrase ~을 것이다 signifies the speaker's volition for verbs with a first-person subject, or potentiality/probability with the third-person subject as shown below.

In Chinese, adding an adverb "可能会" (probably) to the sentence indicates probability. For volition, the word "要" is used.

In Japanese, "でしょう" signifies probability. However, the speaker's volition is weakened in conversation, expressing it indirectly through "でしょう".

Examples

1. The weather will probably be nice tomorrow.

J 明日はいい天気でしょう。

C 明天天气可能很好。

K 내일 날씨가 좋을 거예요.

2. My roommate will probably go to the party.

J ルームメートはパーティーに行くでしょう。

C 我的室友可能会去参加聚会。

K 제 룸메이트는 파티에 갈 거예요.

3. The teacher probably studied hard at college.

J 先生は大学でよく勉強したでしょう。

C 老师可能在大学里刻苦学习。

K 선생님은 대학교 때 공부를 열심히 하셨을 거예요.

4. A: 내일 날씨가 어때요?

B: 자켓을 입으세요. 내일 추울 거예요. (probability)

A: What's the weather like tomorrow?

B: Please put on your jacket. It will be cold tomorrow.

5. A: 이번 주말에 뭐 할 거예요?

B: 가족하고 영화를 볼 거예요. (volition)

A: What are you going to do this weekend?

B: I'm going to watch a movie with my family.

Exercise

Ask and answer the questions about the probable future in each of the three languages.

(1) What will you do this weekend?

(2) What are you going to do after this class?

(3) What is the weather like tomorrow?

Chinese causative verbs: 叫&让

Causative verbs are used to cause or influence people to do things. In English, verbs like "make", "let", "have", and "get" are typically used. The most common Chinese equivalents are 让(ràng) and 叫(jiào). 叫 typically appears in spoken Chinese (especially in the northern dialect), while 让 is commonly used both in spoken and written Chinese.

1. The teacher let students go home early.

老师让学生早点回家。

2. From a friend to a friend: If you don't know how to do it, get him to teach you. I don't know, either.

要是你不会，叫他教你，我也不会。

3. Drinking tea makes it hard for me to fall asleep.

喝茶让我睡不着。

4. Learning foreign languages makes me happy.

学外文让我很开心。

Exercise

Make a conversation about what your parents often asked you to do when you were young.

A: 你小时候爸妈让你做什么？

B: 他们常常让我__________。

把/将- construction

Sub+把/将+Object+Verb+Complement

The 把/将 construction is unique to the Chinese language. It is used to demonstrate the disposal of the object, and the impact or effect the action has on it.

sub.把+O+V+Complement

Situation 1: A mother is asking her child to finish the food.

妈妈mom：把饭吃了。 全部食べなさい。음식을 다 드세요.

孩子child：不想吃。食べたくない。먹고 싶지 않앙요.

Situation 2: Student A took away student B's book, so B is asking A to give it back.

学生A: 把书给我。本を返して。책을 주세요.

学生B: 等一下吧。 ちょっと待って。잠깐 기다리세요.

Situation 3: Describing a student's action in the classroom.

他把老师说的话写下来。先生が言ったことを書きました。선생님께서 말씀하시는 것을 적었어요. He wrote down what the teacher said.

Japanese Vないで(Verb plain negative form + で) construction

In Japanese, Vないで(Verb plain negative form + で) means "without doing the action".

食べないで (without eating)

見ないで (without teaching)

飲まないで (without drinking)

書かないで (without writing)

行かないで (without going)

しないで (without doing)

朝ごはんを食べないで学校に行った。

(I) went to school without having breakfast.

天気予報を見ないで出かけた。

(I) went out without watching the weather forecast.

時々、教科書を読まないで授業に行く。

(I) sometimes go to class without reading the textbook.

今日はスーパーに行かないで家に帰ります。

(I) will go home without going to the supermarket.

電話しないで友達の家に行きました。

(I) went to my friend's house without calling.

Exercise

Make conversations in the given situations.

A: 大丈夫ですか。

(Are you alright?)

B: 朝ごはんを食べないで来ましたからおなかがすいています。

(I'm hungry because I came here without having breakfast.)

1. A: ____.

B: (I'm sleepy because I studied without going to bed last night.)

2. A: ____.

B: (I'm thirsty because I ran without taking a taxi.)

3. A: ____.

B: (I don't understand the class because I came to class without reading the textbook.)

4. A: ____.

B: (I am worried because I did my presentation without preparation.)

Vないで is also used to make a negative request as in "please do not V".

まだ食べないでください。(Please do not eat yet.)

本を見ないでください。(Please do not look at the book.)

ここではたばこを吸わないでください。あそこで吸ってください。(Please do not smoke here. Please smoke over there.)

09

John/요한복음/约翰福音/ヨハネの福音書

11:25, 26

Jesus said to her, "I am the resurrection and the life. The one who believes in me will live, even though they die; and whoever lives by believing in me will never die. Do you believe this?"

예수께서 마르다에게 말씀하셨다. "나는 부활이요 생명이니, 나를 믿는 사람은 죽어도 살고, 살아서 나를 믿는 사람은 영원히 죽지 않을 것이다. 네가 이것을 믿느냐?"

耶稣对她说：「复活在我，生命也在我。 信我的人虽然死了，
Yēsū duì tā shuō: `Fùhuó zài wǒ, shēngmìng yě zài wǒ. Xìn wǒ de rén suīrán sǐle,
也必复活；凡活着信我的人必永远不死。 你信这话吗？」
yě bì fùhuó; fán huózhe xìn wǒ de rén bì yǒngyuǎn bùsǐ. Nǐ xìn zhè huà ma?'

イエスは彼女(かのじょ)に言わ(いわ)れた、「わたしはよみがえりであり、命(いのち)である。わたしを信じる(しんじる)者(もの)は、たとい死ん(しん)でも生きる(いきる)。また、生き(いき)ていて、わたしを信じる(しんじる)者(もの)は、いつまでも死な(しな)ない。あなたはこれを信じる(しんじる)か」。

Common Words

耶稣, イエス, 예수: Jesus

她, 彼女, 그녀: she

说, いう [言う], 말하다: to say

复活, よみがえり, 부활: resurrection

生命, いのち [命], 생명: life

死, しぬ [死ぬ], 죽다: to die

活, いきる [生きる], 살다: to live

永远, いつまでも, 영원히: forever

信, 信じる [しんじる], 믿다: to believe

这, これ, 이것: this

Chinese

对: to, に, 에게

也: also, やっぱり, 역시

虽然: although, かりに [仮に], 비록

着: continuous aspect marker, 지속상 접사

Japanese

者: man, 人 [rén], 사람

たとい: although, 虽然, 비록

いつまでも: forever, 언제까지나

Korean

말씀하시다: to say (honorific), 说 [shuō], いう [言う]

느냐: interrogative ending to inferior person (archaic style)

Concessive construction: 虽然，でも，어/아도

When a situation is expected to happen regardless of what occurs in an adverse situation, concessive grammar structure shall be used. In Chinese, the adverb 虽然 is placed at the beginning of a sentence, which is typically followed by 但是/可是(but) clause. For example,

Although I'm tired, (but) I am still working.
虽然我很累，可是我还在工作。
Although I don't have much money, (but) I am happy.
虽然我的钱不多，可是我很幸福。

In Japanese, てform + も is used.
The forms are as follows:
Verbs:

るverbs; change る to て (食べる→食べて、見る→見て)

うverbs ending with

う、つ、る　って　会う→会って、待つ→待って、分かる→分かって)

む、ぶ、ぬ　んで　(読む→読んで、遊ぶ→遊んで、死ぬ→死んで)

く　　　　　いて　(書く→書いて)

ぐ　　　　　いで　(泳ぐ→泳いで)

す　　　　　して　(話す→話して)

Exception: 行く→行って (only て form)

する→して

来る→来て

いAdjectives: take out the い and replace it with くても

なAdjectives: add でも

Nouns: add でも

The Korean 어/아도 is conjugated with the predicate's stem in the first clause.

먹다 → 먹어도, 보다 → 보아도, 공부하다 → 공부해도, 학생이다 → 학생이라도

■ Examples

1. Even though my friend didn't have time, he exercised.

C 虽然我的朋友没有时间，但是他还是锻炼身体。

J 時間がなくても(時間がなかったのに라고 주로 말한다)運動しました。

K 시간이 없어도, 내 친구는 운동을 했어요.

2. Although it rains tomorrow, I'll go to the beach.

C 虽然明天下雨，我还是会去海边。

J 雨が降ってもビーチに行きます。

K 내일 비가 와도 바닷가에 갈 거예요.

Exercise

Create sentences combining two situations in three languages.

to take medicine 吃药	to not be better 没好
to make a phone call 打电话	to not pick up the phone 接电话
to sleep late 晚睡	to get up early 早起
to be sick 生病	to go to school 去学校
to be spicy 辣	to be able to eat 吃

Expressions

Korean honorific subject particle 께서 and honorific target/source particle 께

Korean sentences can hardly be uttered without the speaker's approximate knowledge of his/her social relationship with the addressee and referent in terms of age category, social status, kinship, in or out-groupness, and/or social situation. The grammatical pattern of Korean honorifics seems to be the most systematic among all known languages.
께서 is the honorific particle for the subject particle 이/가 (refer to Lesson 2), and 께 is used to indicate the target and the source.

My grandmother lives in Korea.
할머니께서 한국에 사세요.

I received a sweater from my grandmother as a gift.
할머니께 스웨터를 선물로 받았어요.

I made a phone call to my grandmother.
어제 할머니께 전화를 드렸어요.

Exercise

Ask three people in the classroom what they got last Christmas.

着 continuous aspect marker in Chinese

As you may have already realized, the Chinese language does not have verb conjugation. Instead, notional words and particles are used to indicate tense and aspect. 着 is an aspect marker that is added to the end of verbs to indicate the continuous aspect in Chinese. It is generally used to describe static actions. E.g.

Examples

The teacher is standing and the students are sitting.
老师站着，学生坐着。

The person is holding a book. 那个人拿着一本书。

I listen to music while reading books. 我听着音乐看书。

Exercise

Describe the actions of the people you see in the picture:

1. Suggested verbs: 站 zhàn, stand 坐 zuò, sit

2. Suggested verb: 拿 ná, hold

3. Suggested verb: 抱 bào, hold sth. in one's arms

4. Suggested verb: 躺 tǎng, lie (down)

10

John/요한복음/约翰福音/ヨハネの福音書

14:6

Jesus answered, "I am the way and the truth and the life. No one comes to the Father except through me."

예수께서 대답하셨다. "내가 곧 길이요 진리요 생명이다. 나로 말미암지 않고서는 아무도 아버지께로 올 사람이 없다."

耶稣说:「我就是道路、真理、生命; 若不借着我,
Yēsū shuō: `Wǒ jiùshì dàolù, zhēnlǐ, shēngmìng; ruò bù jièzhe wǒ,
没有人能到父那里 去。
méiyǒu rén néng dào fù nàlǐ qù.

イエスは彼(かれ)に言(い)われた、「わたしは道(みち)であり、真理(しんり)であり、命(いのち)である。だれでもわたしによらないでは、父(ちち)のみもとに行(い)くことはできない。

Common Words

道路, みち [道], 길: way

真理, しんり [真理], 진리: truth

借, よる [依る], 의지하다: to depend on

到: to come, くる [来る], 오다

去: to go, いく [行く], 가다

Chinese

若: if, もし [若し], 만약

能: cam, could, かのう [可能], 가능하다

那里: there, そこ, 거기

Japanese

彼: he, 他 [tā], 그

だれでも: whoever, 无论是谁 [wúlùnshìshéi], 누구든지

みもとに: side (honorific), 곁(존대 표현)

できない: to be unable to, …不起 [… · buqǐ], ~을 수 없다

Korean

대답하다: to answer, 回答 [huídá], こたえる [答える]

말미암다: to be derived from, 经过 [jīngguò], へる [経る]
아무도: no one, 某 [mǒu], だれそれ [誰某]

Conditional Sentences: 如果/要是 (rúguǒ / yàoshì), ～たら，~으면 If…

The conjunction 若 is used in classical Chinese or written/formal language to introduce a conditional sentence in Chinese. In modern spoken Chinese, 如果/要是 is most commonly used to introduce this type of sentence. Its meaning and use are similar to the English "if". The only difference lies in the word order. In Chinese, 要是/如果 is always placed at the beginning of sentence, with 就 sometimes used in the second clause to mean "then".

The most versatile conditional form in Japanese is ～たら。 The pattern is as follows.

Verbs:

Ru-verbs (affirmative) change the last syllable る to たら as in 食べたら、見たら

(negative) change the last syllable る to なかったら

U-verbs ending with ぬ、ぶ、む → (affirmative) んだら (死んだら、遊んだら、読んだら)

ending with つ、う → (affirmative) ったら(待ったら、買ったら)
ending with く → (affirmative) いたら(書いたら)
ending with ぐ → (affirmative) いだら(泳いだら)
ending with す → (affirmative) したら(話したら)

(negative) change the last consonant u sound to a sound and add なかったら
(死ななかったら、遊ばなかったら、読まなかったら、待たなかったら、買わなかったら、書かなかったら、泳がなかったら、話さなかったら)

行く (affirmative) 行ったら
(negative) 行かなかったら
する (affirmative) したら
(negative) しなかったら

Adjectives:

I-adjectives: (affirmative) change the last syllable い to かったら (おいしかったら)
(negative) change the last syllable い to くなかったら (おいしくなかったら)
Na-adjectives: (affirmative) add だったら (元気だったら)
(negative) じゃなかったら(元気じゃなかったら)

Nouns: (affirmative) add だったら (学生だったら)

(negative) add じゃなかったら (学生じゃなかったら)

In Korean, the connective ~(으)면 is attached to the predicate stem as a suffix.

1. If you can't find your way, call me.

C 要是找不到路，给我打电话。

J 道が分からなかったら、私に電話してください。

K 길을 찾을 수 없으면, 저한테 전화하세요.

2. If you are free tomorrow, then go to school with me.

C 如果你明天有空，就跟我去学校。

J 明日ひまだったら、いっしょに学校へ行きませんか。

K 내일 시간이 되면, 저하고 같이 학교에 가요.

Exercise

1. Ask and answer the questions with your partner.

a. If you cannot sleep, what do you do?

b. If it rains tomorrow, where will we meet?

c. If the weather is good, what are you going to do?

d. If the homework is hard, what do you do?

2. Make conversation with your partner under the below conditions:

You have a lot of time. 你有很多时间。 ひまです。시간이 많다.

You have a lot of money. 你有很多钱。お金があります。돈이 많다.

You are stressed. 你压力很大。ストレスがあります。스트레스를 받다.

Chinese Directional Verb Complement 来/去

来 and 去 are commonly used as verbs in Chinese to mean come and go. However, they are also commonly used as verb complements to indicate the direction of the action. 来 indicates the action is moving towards the speaker, whereas 去 indicates moving away from the speaker. Take the sentence in the Bible as an example: "没有人能到父那里去". 去 is placed after the verb and object to show that the Father is currently at another location and that He is away from us. Therefore, we shall say "go" to him, rather than have the Father "come" to us.

Japanese has a very similar concept of "go" and "come" to indicate the direction of an action. The phrases 行く and 来る are often used with another verb such as 帰ってくる (return to the speaker's direction)、持っていく (take something to the direction away from the speaker).

In Korean, the serial verb construction is used in a similar manner. As shown in 3), the Chinese 回+ 去 has the exact structure as in Korean serial verbs 돌다 to turn + 가다 to go, which is connected as 돌아가다 with the help of the connector “아”.

1. A and B are neighbors. They just ran into each other on the street.

A: Where are you going?

C 你上哪儿去？

J どこに行きますか。

K 어디에 가세요?

B: I am going to get groceries.

C 我买菜去。

J 買い物に行きます。

K 장보러 가요.

2. A is the tenant, and B is the mover.

A (in the room): Can you help me move the TV in?

C 帮把电视搬进来吧。

J テレビを中に持って来てください。

K 텔레비전을 옮기는 것을 도와줄래요?

B (outside the room): It’s too heavy. I can’t move it in.

C 太重了，我搬不进去。

J 重すぎます。持って行けません。

K 너무 무거워요. 옮길 수 없어요.

3. A is B's classmate. They are currently in school.

They are talking about their plans for Thanksgiving.

A: When are you going back?

C 你什么时候回去？

J いつ帰りますか。

K 언제 (집으로) 돌아가요?

B: I am going back on November the 28th.

C 我11月28号回去。

J 11月28日に帰ります。

K 11월 28일에 돌아가요.

Simple Directional Verbs								
Directional Verbs		上 to ascend	下 to descend	进（進） to enter	出 to exit	回 to return	过（過） to cross	起 to rise,lift
Directional Complements	来	上来 come up 上がってくる 올라오다	下来 come down 下がってくる 내려오다	进来 come into 入ってくる 들어오다	出来 come out 出てくる 나오다	回来 come back 帰ってくる 돌아오다	过来 come over (やって)来る 지나오다	起来 lift sth. up
	去	上去 go up 上がっていく 올라가다	下去 go down 下がっていく 내려가다	进去 go into 入っていく 들어가다	出去 go out 出ていく 나가다	回去 go back 帰っていく 돌아가다	过去 go over いく 지나가다	

Exercise

Fill in the blanks with the appropriate directional verb-complement words from the above table.

Let's go up and take a look.

我们__________看看。

Come up!

你快__________!

The weather is so nice. Let's go out and take a walk.

天气真好! 我们__________走走。

Come in! It's cold outside.

快__________! 外面很冷。

Korean Indefinite Pronoun 아무도

아무도 is a pronoun that refers to "nobody". It is a negative polarity item which involves a negation in the sentence, unlike in English. Also, it does not take either the subject particles(이/가) or the object particles(을/를) as shown below. However, the "to" particle 에게/한테 and "with" particle "하고" can be inserted between 아무 and 도.

1. I didn't meet anybody last weekend.

- **K** 지난 주말에 아무도 만나지 않았어요.
- **C** 我上个星期谁都没见。
- **J** 先週に誰も会わなかった。

2. Nobody was not at home.

- **K** 아무도 집에 없었어요.
- **C** 谁都不在家。
- **J** 誰も家にいない。

3. I didn't say that to anybody.

- **K** 아무에게도 말하지 않았어요.
- **C** 我谁都没说。
- **J** 誰にも言わなかった。

In Chinese, questions pronouns such as 谁(who)、什么(what)、什么时候(when)、哪里(where)、and 哪个(which) are used to express the meaning of "every, any" or "nothing, no one". The positive structure is Question Pronoun + 都 + Verb, and the negative structure is Question Pronoun + 都 + 不/没+Verb. When there is a subject, it can either go before the question pronoun or after.

The Japanese structure for this is wh-question words + も, and negative ending such as だれも教室にいない (meaning "no one is in the classroom"). The particle も replaces は、が、を but not others (だれにも言わなかった).

Exercise

Imagine you just arrived in a new country. What would it be like?

- I don't know anyone.
- I haven't talked to anyone.
- Nobody looks the same as me.
- No one can speak my language.
- Nobody can understand me.

11

John/요한복음/约翰福音/ヨハネの福音書

17:3

Now this is eternal life: that they know you, the only true God, and Jesus Christ, whom you have sent.

영생은 오직 한 분이신 참 하나님을 알고 또 아버지께서 보내신 예수 그리스도를 아는 것입니다.

认识你一独一的真神，并且认识你所差来的耶稣基督，
Rènshí nǐ— dú yī de zhēnshén, bìngqiě rènshí nǐ suǒ chà lái de yēsū jīdū,
这就是永生。
zhè jiùshì yǒngshēng.

永遠(えいえん)の命(いのち)とは、唯一(ゆいいつ)の、まことの神(かみ)でいますあなたと、また、あなたがつかわされたイエス・キリストとを知(し)ることであります。

Common Words

认识: to know, 知る [しる], 알다

独一: only, ゆいいつ [唯一] , 오직

真: true, まこと, 참

并且: and, また, 또

差来: to send, おくる [送る], 보내다

Chinese

这: this, これ, 이것

就: a advers to affirm the statement

Japanese

永遠: eternal, 永远 [yǒngyuǎn], 영원

知る: to know, 认识 [rèn · shi], 알다

Korean

영생: eternal life, 永生 [yǒngshēng], えいせい [永生]

분: person (honorific)

Adjective modifying a noun

In Chinese, when a disyllabic adjective modifies a noun or noun phrase, the particle 的 is inserted in between. In Japanese and Korean, words are conjugated to become adjectives.

In Japanese, adjectives come before a noun to modify it. Na-adjectives require な before the noun, whereas i-adjectives simply precede the noun with no modification.

In Korean, the suffix ~(으)ㄴ is attached to the adjective stem, ~은 for the consonant ending stem and ~ㄴ for the vowel ending stem (밝다 to be bright + 은 = 밝은, 피곤하다 to be tired + ㄴ = 피곤한). However, adjectives that end with 있다 or 없다 such as 재미있다 and 맛있다 take ~는 as the modifier. Below is a table to help you understand how adjectives are used in each of the three languages.

Chinese	Korean	Japanese	English
漂亮的女孩	예쁜 소녀	かわいい女の子	Pretty girl
舒服的床	편한 침대	心地よいベッド	Comfortable bed
便宜的东西	싼 물건	安い物	Cheap stuff
好看的电视	재미있는 TV 쇼	よいテレビ番組	Good TV show

Connecting words and sentences

Unlike English, where the versatile conjunction "and" can be used in all cases to connect nouns, adjectives, adverbs, verbs, phrases, and sentences, Chinese uses "和" (and), Korean 와/과/하고, and Japanese "と" to connect nouns or noun phrases as explained in L3. No specific words are used to connect all of the various types of words and sentences. Instead, a comma would perform such functions. However, in formal Chinese, 并且 can be used to connect sentences as shown in the Bible verse above.

For the connection of complete sentences, Korean uses the conjunction 그리고 or the connective ~고 with conjugation.

In Japanese, the て form is used to connect adjectives and sentences.

For example:

1. I bought a comfortable bed and a cheap TV.

C 我买了舒服的床和便宜的电视。

K 편한 침대와/하고 싼 텔레비전을 샀어요.

J 心地のいいベッドと安いテレビを買いました。

2. The bed I bought is both comfortable and cheap.

C 我买的床很舒服、很便宜。

K 제가 산 침대는 편하고 싸요.

J 私が買ったベッドは心地よくて安いです。

3. I read the book word by word, sentence by sentence at an average pace.

C 我一字一句、不快不慢地读书。

K 저는 한 단어 한 단어 읽어요. 빠르지 않고 느리지 않게 책을 읽어요.

J 普通のスピードで本を一語一語、一文一文、読みました。

4. I bought some cheap stuff, and had some food before I went back home.

C 我买了便宜的东西，吃了点饭，然后回家。

K 집에 오기 전에 싼 물건을 사고 밥을 먹었어요.

J うちに帰る前に、安い物を買って食べました。

5. Know what you are doing, and know why you are doing it.

C 知道自己正在做的事情，并且知道你这样做的原因。

K 자신이 무슨 일을 하는지를 알고 왜 하는지를 아세요.

J 自分が何をしているか、そして、どうしてそれをしているのか知りなさい。

Japanese phrases giving a definition or interpretation

Noun/Noun phraseとはNoun/Noun phraseのことである
(giving a definition)

1. NYUとはニューヨーク大学のことです。(NYU is New York University.)
2. コンビニとはコンビニエンスストアのことです。(コンビニ means convenience store.)
3. 留学とは外国で勉強することです。(留学 means study abroad.)

Numbers

The three languages have numeration systems with words that correspond to the numbers zero to nine. Similarly to the number system in English, the system also has special words to represent ten, a hundred, a thousand, ten thousand, as well as other multiples of ten. Both Japanese and Korean use two sets of numbers: Sino numbers and native numbers.

0	零	零れい・ゼロ	영
1	一	一いち	일
2	二	二に	이
3	三	三さん	삼

4	四	四よん	사
5	五	五ご	오
6	六	六ろく	육
7	七	七しち・なな	칠
8	八	八はち	팔
9	九	九きゅう	구

To make bigger numbers, you can combine the numbers above with the special counters as shown below.

10	十	十じゅう	십
100	一百	百ひゃく	백
1,000	一千	千せん	천
10,000	一万	万まん	만
100,000	十万	十万じゅうまん	억

11 is "ten one", 12 is "ten two" and so on. 20 is "two ten", 21 is "two ten one", and so on up to 99. All three languages differ from English in that there is a specific word for ten thousand, 万 wàn / 万 man / 만.

17	十七	十七じゅうしち・じゅうなな	십칠
25	二十五	二十五にじゅうご	이십오
239	二百三十九	二百三十九にひゃくさんじゅうきゅ・にひゃくさんじゅうく	이백삼십구
8,436	八千四百三十六	八千四百三十六はっせんよんひゃくさんじゅうろく	팔천사백삼십육
62,490	六万二千四百九十	六万二千四百九十ろくまんにせんよんひゃくきゅうじゅう	육만이천사백구십
10,101	一万零一百零一	一万百一いちまんひゃくいち	만백일

*** Note that, in Chinese, when you say "one hundred", "one thousand", and "ten thousand", "一" must be used before 百，千，万。 In contrast, in Korean, 일 is omitted before those words.

Exercise

● Read the following numbers in each of the three languages.

2893

39402

932890

- Ask and answer the questions with your partner as in the example.

A: How much is it? 얼마예요?

B: It's $ 580. 오백팔십불이에요.

DOLLAR 49,320

RMB 1050

YEN 9870

WON 12400

Japanese and Korean Native Numbers

1	ひい	하나
2	ふう	둘
3	みい	셋
4	よう	넷
5	いつ	다섯
6	むう	여섯
7	なな	일곱

8	やあ	여덟
9	ここ	아홉
10	とお	열

Noun counters

When counting, you should be mindful of the different counters in all three languages. Nouns are classified into many groups depending on shape or kind. Note the difference in order between the languages.

Three books	三本书	책 세 권	三冊 (양사로만 사용)
Two bowls of rice	两 * 碗米饭	밥 두 그릇	二杯 (양사로만 사용)
Four cups of coffee	四杯咖啡	커피 세 잔	四杯 (양사로만 사용)
Five chairs	五把椅子	의자 다섯 개	五脚 (다리 있는 의자만 , 소파 제외)
Six people	六个人	사람 여섯 명	六人
Seven dogs	七只狗	개 일곱 마리	七匹

* Note that when counting objects, 二 (two) is replaced with 两 (two). For example, 两本书(two books), 两杯咖啡(two cups of coffee).

* Note that in Japanese specific items must be indicated. For

example, 二冊 can be two magazines, dictionaries, or other similar items besides books.

Exercise

Please count how many objects/people are there in the room.

______个中国人/韩国人/日本人/美国人______Chinese/Korean/Japanese/American

____杯咖啡 ____cups of coffee

____支笔 ____pens

____个学生 ____students

____本书 ____books

12

John/요한복음/约翰福音/ヨハネの福音書
20:31

But these are written that you may believe that Jesus is the Messiah, the Son of God, and that by believing you may have life in his name.

그런데 여기에 이것이나마 기록한 목적은 여러분으로 하여금 예수가 그리스도요 하나님의 아들이심을 믿게 하고, 또 그렇게 믿어서 그의 이름으로 생명을 얻게 하려는 것이다.

但记这些事要叫你们信耶稣是基督，　是神的儿子，
Dàn jì zhèxiē shì yào jiào nǐmen xìn yēsū shì jīdū, shì shén de érzi,
并且叫你们信了他，　就可以因他的名得生命。
bìngqiě jiào nǐmen xìnle tā, jiù kěyǐ yīn tā de míng dé shēngmìng.

しかし、これらのことを書(か)いたのは、あなたがたがイエスは神(かみ)の子(こ)キリストであると信(しん)じるためであり、また、そう信(しん)じて、イエスの名(な)によって命(いのち)を得(え)るためである。

Common Words

记, かく [書く], 기록하다: to write

这些, これら, 이것: these

因, 因る [よる], 인하다/으로: to be caused

生命, 命[いのち], 생명: life

得, 得る [える], 얻다: to gain

Chinese

但: but, ただし [但し], 다만

事: thing, こと, 일

叫: to make, させる, 하도록 하다

并且: and, そして (また), 그리고 (또한)

可以: can/may, できる [出来る], 할 수 있다

Japanese

しかし: but, 却, 그러나

あなたがた: you (plural), 你们, 여러분

そう: such, 那么, 그렇게

Korean

그런데: by the way, 可是, ところで

여기: here, 这儿, ここ

목적: purpose, 目的, もくてき [目的]

그렇게: such, 那么, そう

Korean perfective noun modifier ~(으)ㄴ

As shown in L7, Korean noun modifiers are diverse depending on certain aspects of the sentence. 는 is used to express a habitual or incomplete event in the relative clause, whereas here ~(으)ㄴ indicates that the event is completed and stays in a resultant state. You may observe that a Korean adjective that modifies a noun takes the identical form ~(으)ㄴ because the adjective describes a state.

여기에 기록한(vs. 기록하는) 목적은 생명을 얻게 하려는 것이다.
The goal that (I) wrote (vs. am writing) is to make you have life.

종업원이 먹은(vs. 먹는) 그릇을 치웠다.
The waiter cleared the bowl that I had eaten (vs. was eating).

Exercise

Complete the following sentences as in the example.

1. A movie that I watched last night.
어제 밤 본 영화
어제 밤 본 영화가 정말 재미있었어요.

2. A food that I cooked.

3. A book that I bought.

4. My roommate that I met.

5. A picture that my old brother took.

Activity

Talk about your travel story by using the noun-modifying structure ~(으)ㄴ + Noun with your classmates. Ask and answer about the country you traveled to, especially the food you ate, the person(s) you went with, the activities that you tried, and the place(s) you went to, etc.

Chinese adverb 就

就 is a very versatile adverb in Chinese. In this lesson, 就 connects two phrases and sentences to mean "in that case," or "then."
The corresponding structure for 就 can be the conditional connective ~(으)면 in Korean.

1. If you are not there, I will not come.
C 要是你不在，我就不来。
K 거기에 없으면 저도 안 갈 거예요..

2. (Since) you don't want to eat, then don't eat.
C 你不想吃，就别吃了。
K 먹고 싶지 않으면 먹지 마세요.

Exercise

Create sentences combining the two.

1. To be sleepy / to drink coffee
2. To be hot / to turn on the air conditioner
3. To be hungry / to eat something
4. To be boring / to watch TV

5. To be cold / to wear clothes

Activity

Make questions and answers using the following grammar items.

1. What do you do while taking a shower?
2. What do you do when you see food on your friend's face?
3. What do you do if you don't have your wallet in a restaurant?
4. What do you do if you really want to drink wine, but there is no wine opener?

Japanese て form

One of the functions of the て form is to connect words and sentences.

Connecting words:

広くてきれいな部屋 (spacious and clean room) 넓고 깨끗한 방
にぎやかで楽しいパーティー (lively and fun party) 활기차고 재밌는 파티
大学の二年生で日本語専攻 (sophomore and Japanese major) 대

학 2학년이고 일본어 전공

Sequences of action:

うちへ帰って、寝ました。(I went home and slept.) 집에 가서 잠을 잤어요.

朝起きて、窓を開けます。(I wake up in the morning and open the windows.) 아침에 일어나서 창문을 열어요.

Manner of action:

歩いて大学に行きます。(I walk to the university = go to the university by walking.) 걸어서 대학교에 가요.

漢字は何回も書いて覚えます。(I memorize kanji by writing them many times.) 한자를 여러 번 써서 외워요.

Reason:

安くていいです。(It's cheap and (so) good.) 싸서 좋아요.

ねぼうして遅刻しました。(I overslept and was late.) 늦잠을 자서 늦었어요.

約束を忘れてすみませんでした。(I am sorry for forgetting the appointment = I forgot the appointment and am sorry. 약속을 잊어서 죄송해요.

Verbs:

Ru-verbs (affirmative) change the last syllable る to て as in 食べ

たら、見たら

U-verbs ending with ぬ、ぶ、む → (affirmative) んで (死んで、遊んで、読んで)

ending with つ、う → (affirmative) って(待って、買って)

ending with く → (affirmative) いて(書いて)

ending with ぐ → (affirmative) いで(泳いで)

ending with す → (affirmative) して(話して)

行く (affirmative) 行って

する (affirmative) して

Adjectives:

I-adjectives: (affirmative) change the last syllable い to くて(おいしくて)

Na-adjectives: (affirmative) add だったら(元気で)

Nouns: (affirmative) add だったら(学生で)

Activity

Talk to each other about what you did yesterday using the Japanese て, Korean 어/아서, and Chinese serial verbs.

13

Acts/사도행전/使徒行传/使徒の働き

1:8

But you will receive power when the Holy Spirit comes on you; and you will be my witnesses in Jerusalem, and in all Judea and Samaria, and to the ends of the earth."

그러나 성령이 너희에게 내리시면, 너희는 능력을 받고, 예루살렘과 온 유대와 사마리아에서, 그리고 마침내 땅 끝에까지 이르러 내 증인이 될 것이다.

但圣灵降临在你们身上，　　你们就必得着能力，
Dàn shènglíng jiànglín zài nǐmen shēnshang, nǐmen jiù bìděizhe nénglì,
并要在耶路撒冷、 犹太全地，　和撒马利亚，
bìng yào zài yēlùsālěng, yóutài quán de, hé sā mǎlìyǎ,
直到地极，作我的见证。
zhídào dì jí,　zuò wǒ de jiànzhèng.

ただ、聖霊(せいれい)があなたがたにくだる時(とき)、あなたがたは力(ちから)を受け(うけ)て、エルサレム、ユダヤとサマリヤの全土(ぜんど)、さらに地(ち)のはてまで、わたしの証(あかし)人(ひと)となるであろう」。

Common Words

但, ただし [但し], 그러나: but

圣灵, せいれい [聖霊], 성령: Holy Spirit

降临, くだる, 내리다: to come down

能力, 力[ちから], 능력: power

耶路撒冷, エルサレム, 예루살렘: Jerusalem

犹太, ユダヤ, 유대: Judea

全地, ぜんど [全土], 온 땅: entire land

撒马利亚, サマリヤ, 사마리아: Samaria

直到, まで, 까지: until

见证, しょうにん [証人], 증인: witness

Chinese

在: at, に, 에

身上: body, み [身], 몸

和: and, および [及び], 그리고

地极: earth pole, りょうきょく [両極], 양극

Japanese

時: time, 时候 [shí·hou], 때

受ける: to receive, 受 [shòu], 받다
さらに [更に]: even, 且兼 [qiějiān], 더욱 더

Korean

받다: to receive, 受 [shòu], うける [受ける]
온: entire, 全 [quán], すべての
에서: from, 自 [zì], から
마침내: at last, 终于 [zhōngyú], ついに [遂に]
이르다: to arrive, 到 [dào], 至る [いたる]
되다: to become, 成为 [chéngwéi], なる [為る]

Korean Subject Honorific ~시

The Korean language can hardly be uttered without the speaker's approximate knowledge of his social relationship with his addressee and referent in terms of age category, social status, and kinship. There are three kinds of honorifics in Korean: subject honorific, listener honorific, and object honorific. The subject honorific -(으)시 is added to a stem when the speaker wants to show his/her respect toward the subject.

The conjugated suffix ~(으)세요 is an honorific form of ~어요/아요. It is a combination of ~(으)시 + ~어요/아요.

Chinese in general does not have conjugations for honorifics. No matter whom you speak with or speak about, the language is the same. There is only one exception – when speaking with someone who has seniority over the speaker, 您 (nín) is used instead of 你 to show respect and politeness. However, 你 can still be used if the speaker and the listener have a very close relationship.

In a formal situation, when speaking about someone who has a higher social standing, someone who is older than you, or someone you don't know very well, honorifics are used in Japanese. The usage of honorifics shifts depending on who you are talking to and about in different situations. For example, you do not use honorifics to talk to or about your own family members. To the contrary, in professional settings, you should use honorifics to speak to or about your superior in the office. However, if someone outside of your own circle (office, company, etc.) comes in, you should use honorifics with the outsider but humble expressions to your superior.

Honorific verbs:

1) These are some most commonly used honorific verbs.

いる→いらっしゃる・いらっしゃいます

行く →いらっしゃる・いらっしゃいます

来る →いらっしゃる・いらっしゃいます

見る → ご覧になる・ご覧になります

言う →おっしゃる・おっしゃいます

する →なさる・なさいます

食べる →召し上がる・召し上がります

飲む →召し上がる・召し上がります

くれる → くださる・くださいます

寝る → お休みになる・お休みになります

知る → ご存知だ・ご存知です

～ている →～ていらっしゃる・～ていらっしゃいます

● 部長は明日アメリカにいらっしゃいます。
(The section manager will go to the US tomorrow.)
부장은 내일 미국으로 가십니다.

● お飲み物は何を召し上がりますか。
(What would you like to drink?)
음료수로 무엇을 드시겠습니까?

2) Other than the verbs above, 「お+verb stem+になる・なります」is used.

教える→お教えになる・なります

買う→お買いになる・なります

● 先生はこの本をお書きになりました。
(The teacher wrote this book.)
선생님께서 책을 쓰셨어요.

Copula だ → でいらっしゃる

● 失礼ですが、山田さんでいらっしゃいますか。
(Excuse me, are you Mr. Yamada?)
실례합니다만 야마다 씨 되십니까?

Adjectives & Nouns:

忙しい→お忙しい
寂しい→お寂しい
好き→お好き
嫌い→お嫌い
家族→ご家族
両親→ご両親
飲み物→お飲み物
食事→お食事

お客様は6時にお食事をなさいます。お魚がお好きですから、おすしがいいでしょう。それから、ミュージカルにいらっしゃいます。

When the Holy Spirit comes on you, you will be my witnesses.

K 성령이 내리시면 내 증인이 될 것이다.

C 但圣灵降临在你们身上，你们会作我的见证。

J 聖霊があなた方にくだる時、あなたの証人となるであろう。

K A: 한국 음식을 좋아하세요?

B: 네, 좋아해요. 저는 갈비를 좋아해요.

C A: 你喜欢韩国菜吗？

B: 喜欢，我喜欢韩式牛仔骨。

J A: 韓国料理がお好きですか。

B: はい、カルビが好きです。

K A: 선생님이 어떠세요?

B: 선생님이 좋으세요.

C A: 你的老师怎么样？

B: 他不错。

J A: 先生はどうですか。

B: いいです。

First meeting in a business setting:

K A: 중국 사람이세요?

B: 아니요, 일본 사람이에요.

C A: 您是中国人吗？

B: 不是，是日本人。

J A: 中国の方でいらっしゃいますか。

B: いいえ、日本人です。

Chinese complement: location

In general, location phrases are placed before verbs in Chinese. However, when describing a change of location that ends in a specific place, we need to place the location phrase after the verb. 到、在 or other verb complements are used to connect the verb and the location.
In Korean, there are the goal/target particles such as 에게/한테/께 for animate nouns and 에 for inanimate objects.

1. When the Holy Spirit comes on you, you will be my witnesses.

C 但圣灵降临在你们身上，你们会作我的见证。

J 聖霊があなた方にくだる時、あなたの証人となるであろう。

K 성령께서 너에게 내리시면, 내 증인이 될 것이다.

2. Who will send him to school today?

C A: 今天谁送他到学校？

B: 我来送。I will do.

J A: 誰が学校に連れて行きますか。

B: 私が連れて行きます。

K A: 오늘 누가 학교에 (그를) 보낼 거예요?

B: 제가 보낼게요.

3. Please help me move the TV to the table.

C A: 请帮我把电视搬到桌子上。

B: 没问题。No problem.

J A: テレビをテーブルに持っていくのを手伝ってください。

B: はい。

K A: 텔레비전을 테이블에 옮기는 것을 도와 주세요.

B: 네, 그래요.

4. Where did I put my cell phone?

C A: 我的手机放在哪儿了？

B: 放在包里了。In your bag.

J A: 私の携帯電話をどこにおきましたか。

B: 鞄の中ですよ。

K A: (제가) 핸드폰을 어디에 두었죠?

B: 가방에 넣었잖아요.

Japanese temporal clause ～時（とき）When~

To describe when something happens or happened, 「時」is used. For the temporal connective, the '~을 때' occurs after verb/adjective conjugation in Korean.

In Chinese, "……的时候" is used to indicate when something happens or happened. In general, there is no difference between present tense and past tense. However, the time phrase 以前 (before) can be added to the sentence if one wants to stress a past habit.

1) Present tense 時～

adjectives/nouns:

忙しい時 (When I am busy) 바쁠 때 我忙的时候

暑い時 (When it is hot) 더울 때 热的时候

暇な時 (When I have free time) 한가할 때 我有空的时候

学生の時 (When I am a student) 학생일 때 我是学生的时候

Verbs: present tense indicates the action is not completed yet.

勉強する時 (When I study) 공부할 때 我学习的时候

ごはんを食べる時 (When I eat) 밥 먹을 때 我吃饭的时候

買い物する時 (When I shop) 쇼핑할 때 我买东西的时候
映画を見る時 (When I watch a movie) 영화를 볼 때 我看电影的时候

2) Past tense 時~

忙しかった時 (When I was busy) 바빴을 때 我忙的时候
暑かった時 (When it was hot) 더웠을 때 热的时候
暇だった時 (When I had free time) 한가했을 때 我有空的时候
学生だった時 (When I was a student) 학생이었을 때 我是学生的时候

Verbs: past tense indicates the action is already completed.

勉強した時 (When I studied - completed studying) 공부했을 때 我学完的时候
ごはんを食べた時 (When I ate - completed eating) 밥 먹었을 때 我吃完饭的时候
おなかがすいた時 (When I am hungry) 배가 고팠을 때 我饿的时候
朝、起きた時 (When I wake up) 아침에 일어났을 때 我醒的时候

- 学校へ行く時電車に乗ります。
  (When I go to school - on the way to school, I take the train.)
  학교에 갈 때 전철을 타요. 我上学的时候，坐地铁。

- 学校へ行く時電車に乗りました。

(When I went to school - on the way to school, I took the train.)

학교에 갈 때 전철을 탔어요. 我以前上学的时候，坐地铁。

- 学校へ行った時、山田さんに会います。

  (When I go to school- at school, I (will) meet Yamada.)

  학교에 가서 야마다를 만나요. 我在学校的时候，会见到山田先生。

- 学校へ行った時、山田さんに会いました。

  (When I went to school - at school, I met Yamada.)

  학교에 가서 야마다를 만났어요. 我以前上学的时候，认识了山田先生。

- When I wake up, I brush my teeth.

  일어날 때 이를 닦아요.

  Correct - 朝起きた時、歯をみがきます。 我起床以后刷牙。

  Not correct - 朝起きる時、歯をみがきます。

- When I was hungry, I ate a sandwich.

  배고플 때 샌드위치를 먹었어요.

  Correct - おなかがすいた時、サンドイッチを食べます。 我(以前)饿的时候吃三明治。

  Not correct - おなかがすく時、サンドイッチを食べます。

Exercise

When do you do the following?

1. ______時、手をあらいます。(wash my hands.)

2. ______時、歯をみがきます。(brush my teeth.)

3. ______時、友達に会います。(meet my friend.)

4. ______時、レストランに行きます。(go to a restaurant.)

5. ______時、公園を散歩します。(stroll in the park.)

14

Acts/사도행전/使徒行传/使徒の働き

4:12

Salvation is found in no one else, for there is no other name under heaven given to mankind by which we must be saved.

이 예수 밖에는, 다른 아무에게도 구원은 없습니다. 사람들에게 주신 이름 가운데 우리가 의지하여 구원을 얻어야 할 이름은, 하늘 아래에 이 이름 밖에 다른 이름이 없습니다.

除他以外，别无拯救；　因为在天下人间，

Chú tā yǐwài, bié wú zhěngjiù; yīnwèi zài tiānxià rénjiān,

没有赐下别的名，　我们可以靠着 得救。

méiyǒu cì xià bié de míng, wǒmen kěyǐ kàozhe déjiù.

この人(ひと)による以外(いがい)に救(すく)いはない。わたしたちを救い(すく)いうる名(な)は、これを別(べつ)にしては、天下(てんか)のだれにも与(あた)えられていないからである。

Common Words

除~以外, いがい [以外], 밖에는 (외에는) : except for, or in addition to

拯救, すくう [救う], 구원: salvation

名, な [名], 이름: name

赐, 与える [あたえる], 주다: to give

Chinese

别无: not/no other, ない, 없다

因为: because, なぜなら, 왜냐하면

别的: other, べつ [別], 다른

可以: can/may, できる [出来る], 할 수 있다

靠: to depend, もた-れる [靠れる], 기대다

得: to gain, 得る [える], 얻다

Japanese

よる [依る]: to depend on, 借 [jiè], 의지하다

別に: apart, 别 [bié], 구별하여

だれ [誰]: anyone, 谁 [shéi], 누구

Korean

다른: different, 别 [bié], ほか [外·他]

아무: anyone, 谁 [shéi], だれ [誰]

없다: to not have, 无 [wú], ない

가운데: among, 中间 [zhōngjiān], なか [中]

의지하다: to depend on, 借 [jiè], よる [依る]

얻다: to gain, 得 [dé], 得る [える]

除了……以外 in addition to; 말고 except for に加えて、以外

Chinese 除了……以外, Korean 말고, and Japanese 以外 have two different meanings depending on the adverb used in the second clause. It has a negative polarity with 都不, 誰も/何も, 아무(도) and an affirmative meaning with 还, 도 for the the purpose of emphasis. Finally, the Japanese に加えて occurs in the first clause for positive meaning.

■ For example

1. 除了… 以外, … 都不 … except

除了他以外, 我谁都不认识。

I don't know anyone except him.

J 彼以外誰も知りません。

K 그 사람 말고 (저는) 아무도 몰라요.

2. 除了英文以外，我别的语言都不会。

I don't know any languages except English.

J 言語は英語以外何も知りません。

K 영어 말고 (저는) 아무 언어도 할 줄 몰라요.

3. 除了米饭以外，我什么都吃。

I eat everything except rice.

J ご飯以外は全部食べました。

K 밥 말고 (저는) 다 먹어요.

4. 除了… 以外，… 还… in addition to, besides

除了中文以外，我还会说韩文。

In addition to Chinese, I can also speak Korean.

J 中国語以外・に加えて、韓国語を話します。

K 중국어 말고, 한국어도 할 줄 알아요.

5. 我每天除了上课以外，还要工作。

Besides taking class everyday, I also have to work.

J 毎日の授業に加えて(以外)、働かなくてはいけません。

K 매일 수업을 듣는 것 말고, 일도 해야 돼요.

Exercise

Ⅰ. Use the structure above to describe the following situations.

1. Someone's language learning schedule

星期一 月曜日 월요일	星期二 火曜日 화요일	星期三 水曜日 수요일	星期四 木曜日 목요일	星期五 金曜日 금요일
学中文 中国語を勉強 する 중국어를 배우다	学中文	学日文 日本語を勉強 する 일본어를 배우다	学中文	学中文

2. Someone's record of the places he has been to

去过 have been to 가 본 적이 있다			没去过 have not been to 가 본 적이 없다
上海 Shanghai 上海 상하이	东京 Tokyo 東京 도쿄	首尔 Seoul ソウル 서울	别的地方 other places 他の場所 다른 지방

3. Someone's list of the food he doesn't eat.

不吃 does not eat 안 먹다			吃 eat 먹다
米饭 rice ご飯 밥	冰淇淋 ice-cream アイスクリーム 아이스크림	可乐 coke コーラ 콜라	别的东西 other food 他の食べ物 다른 음식

II. Conversation. Ask your partner about the following questions. Answer with the structure above.

1. What language (s) do you know?

C 你会什么语言？

J 何語が分かりますか。

K 어떤 말을 할 줄 알아요?

2. Where have you been?

C 你去过什么地方？

J どこに行ったことがありますか。

K 어디에 가 봤어요?

3. What do you not eat?

C 你不吃什么东西？

J 何を食べませんか。

K 어떤 음식을 안 먹어요?

Japanese passives ~られる、aれる

The passive construction is described from the point of view of the object.

In Korean, the passive suffixes attach to the verb stem for passive expressions such as 보이다 to be seen, 먹히다 to be eaten, 들리다 to be heard, 안기다 to be hugged. Passives are more common in English and Japanese than in Korean, as almost all transitive verbs can be made into passives. In Korean, however, only a limited number of transitive verbs can be made passive. Passives are not common in modern spoken Chinese either, unless the sentence is describing an unpleasant event such as "the wallet is stolen" (钱包被偷了).

Japanese passive forms:

るverbs: replace the last "る" to "られる"

食べる 먹다 → 食べられる 먹히다

見る 보다 → 見られる 보이다

うverbs: replace the last vowel "u" to "a" and add "れる"

書く 쓰다 → 書かれる 쓰이다

待つ 기다리다 → 待たれる 없음

買う 팔다 → 買われる 팔리다

Irregular verbs:

する 하다 → される 하게 되다

来(く)る 오다 → 来(こ)られる 오게 되다

Japanese passive is used mainly in the following situations.

1) Similarly to the English passive form

- 英語は世界中で話される。
  (English is spoken all over the world.)
  영어는 세계에서 사용돼요.
  全世界到处都说英文。

- この公園は1915年につくられた。
  (This park was made in 1915.)
  이 공원은 1915년에 만들어졌어요.
  这个公园是1915年建的。(colloquial/active) 这个公园建于1915年。(formal/passive)

- ニューヨークはビッグアップルと呼ばれる。
  (New York City is called the Big Apple.)
  뉴욕은 빅 애플이라고 불려요.
  纽约又叫做大苹果。(colloquial/active) 纽约被称为大苹果。(formal/passive)

● 先生にほめられた。

(I was praised by my teacher.)

선생님에게 칭찬받았어요.

老师表扬了我。(colloquial/active)　我受到了老师的表扬。(formal/passive)

2) Being inconvenienced by someone's action with the negative implication that the subject is annoyed or bothered by it.

● お母さんに日記を読まれた。

(My mother read my diary.)

(*어머니에게 일기를 읽어졌어요.

妈妈读了我的日记)

어머니가 (제) 일기를 읽으셨어요.

我的日记被妈妈读了。(Passive voice is used here because it's an unpleasant situation.)

● 弟にコンピューターをこわされた。

(My little brother broke my computer.)

(* 동생에게 컴퓨터를 고장내졌어요. 我弟弟弄坏了我的电脑。)

동생이 컴퓨터를 고장냈어요.

我的电脑被弟弟弄坏了。

● お金を盗まれた。

(Someone stole my money.)

돈을 도둑 맞았어요.

我的钱被偷了。

- お母さんにおこられた。

  (My mother got angry at me.)

  어머니에게 일이 생겼어요.

  我妈妈对我很生气。(passive voice is not used here because 生气 is an adjective in this case. Only verbs can be used in Chinese passive voice.)

- 赤ちゃんに泣かれた。

  (The baby cried.)

  아기가 울었어요. (* 아기에게 울어졌어요.)

  孩子哭了。(passive voice is not used here because "cry" is always an action initiated by the subject. However, you can say 孩子被我弄哭了, 'I did something that caused the child to cry'.)

- 雨に降られた。

  (I got rained on.)

  (* 비가 내려졌어요.) 비를 맞았어요.

  我被雨淋了。

3) Honorific use:

● 社長はニューヨークに行かれた。

(The company president went to New York.)

사장님은 뉴욕에 가셨어요.

公司董事长去了纽约。

(There's no use of honorifics in Chinese.)

● お客様は二時にこちらに来られる。

(The guest will come here at 2:00.)

손님은 두 시에 여기에 오셨어요.

客人两点会到。 (There's no use of honorifics in Chinese.)

● 先生は去年この本を書かれた。

(The teacher wrote this book last year.)

선생님은 작년에 이 책을 쓰셨어요.

老师去年写了这本书。

(There's no use of honorifics in Chinese.)

Activity

If a student chooses an active verb, the other gives its passive form and then creates a sentence using it.

Verbs: to open, to listen, to close, to catch, to eat, to see, to read, to hit, to hang….

15

Acts/사도행전/使徒行传/使徒の働き
20:24

However, I consider my life worth nothing to me, if only I may finish the race and complete the task the Lord Jesus has given me--the task of testifying to the gospel of God's grace.

그러나 내가 나의 달려갈 길을 다 달리고, 주 예수께 받은 사명, 곧 하나님의 은혜의 복음을 증언하는 일을 다하기만 하면, 나는 내 목숨이 조금도 아깝게 여기지 않습니다.

我却不以性命为念，　也不看为宝贵，
Wǒ què bù yǐ xìngmìng wéi niàn, yě bùkàn wéi bǎoguì,
只要行完我的路程，
zhǐyào xíng wán wǒde lùchéng,
成就我从主耶稣 所领受的职事，
chéngjiù wǒ cóng zhǔ yēsū suǒ lǐngshòu de zhí shì,
证明 神恩惠的福音。
zhèngmíng shén ēnhuì de fúyīn.

しかし、わたしは自分(じぶん)の行程(こうてい)を走(はし)り終(お)え、主(しゅ)イエスから賜(たま)わった、神(かみ)のめぐみの福音(ふくいん)をあかしする任務(にんむ)を果(はた)し得(え)さえしたら、このいのちは自分(じぶん)にとって、少(すこ)しも惜(お)しいとは思(おも)わない。

Common Words

却, しかし, 그러나: however

性命, いのち, 생명/목숨: life

以…为…, おもう [思う], 여기다: consider…as…

领受, たまわる [賜る], 받다: to be given/ to receive

证明, あかしす, 증언하다: to testify

恩惠, めぐみ, 은혜: grace

福音, ふくいん [福音], 복음: gospel

Chinese

宝贵: precious, とうとい [尊い·貴い], 귀중하다

行完: to finish (the race), かんそうする[完走する], 완주하다

路程: journey, こうてい [行程], 노정

职事: task, にんむ [任務], 일

Japanese

行程: journey, 路程 [lùchéng], 노정

走る: to run, 跑 [pǎo], 달리다

終える: to finish, 完成 [wán//chéng], 마치다

任務: duty, 任务 [rèn wu], 임무

果たす: to complete, 完成 [wán//chéng], 완수하다

少しも: rarely (negative), 丝毫 [sīháo], 조금도

惜しい: to think as a waste, 可惜 [kěxī], 아깝다

Korean

달려가다: to run, 跑 [pǎo], はしる [走る]

다: completely, 都 [dōu], すべて

사명: calling, 使命 [shǐmìng], しめい [使命]

곧: that is, 即 [jí], すなわち

다하다: to finish, 完成 [wán/chéng], おえる [終える]

Source markers (Ablative)

从，~から，~께 (에게서, 한테서, 에서)

These markers express a source from which you receive or hear something, which corresponds to the target markers (See L6). Here the Korean 께 is an honorific form of 에게서 or 한테서 for animate nouns, 에서 for inanimate nouns (ex: place). In Chinese, the preposition word 从 (from) is used for both people and place. Likewise, the Japanese から can be used for time in addition to people and places. For もらう (to receive), からcan be replaced with に。

Examples

1. A: What did you receive for your birthday gift?

K 생일 선물로 뭐 받았어요?

C 你收到了什么生日礼物？

J 誕生日のプレゼントに何をもらいましたか。

B: I received some money from my parents and a book from my friend.

K 부모님께 용돈을 받았어요. 그리고 친구한테서 책을 받았어요.

C 我从父母那里收到了零花钱，从朋友那里收到了一本书。

J 両親からお金をもらって、友達から本をもらいました。

2. A: Where does this sound come from?

K 어디에서 소리가 나요?

C 这个声音是从哪儿来的？

J この音はどこから聞こえてくるの。

B: Oh, it's from upstairs. My friend is playing the guitar.

K 아, 위층에서 나요. 친구가 기타를 치고 있어요.

C 哦，是从楼上来的。我的朋友正在弹吉他。

J 二階からだよ。友達がギターを弾いているんだ。

Exercise

Translate into each language.

1. Linda called her parents yesterday.

2. Linda received a gift from her parents.

3. Linda writes an email to her friend.

4. Linda received an email from her friend.

5. Linda often texted her aunt.

Activity

Ask your classmates what they received last Christmas.

Examples

1. A: What did you get last Christmas?

K 작년 크리스마스에 무슨 선물 받았어요?

C 去年圣诞节你收到了什么礼物？

J 去年のクリスマスに何をもらいましたか。

B: I got shoes and a baseball cap.

K 신발하고 야구 모자를 받았어요.

C 我收到了一双鞋和一顶棒球帽。

J 靴と野球帽をもらいました。

2. A: Who did you get them from?

K 누구한테 받았어요?

C 是从谁那里得到的？(it will be more natural to say: 是谁给你的？)

J 誰からもらいましたか。

B: I got the shoes from my grandmother and the baseball cap from my brother.

K 신발은 할머니께 받았고 야구 모자는 형한테서 받았어요.

C 鞋子是从外婆那里得到的，棒球帽是从我哥哥那里得到的。(it will be more natural to say: 鞋子是外婆送的，棒球帽是哥哥送的。*)

J 靴は祖母からで、野球帽は兄(older brother)からもらいました。

* When the question is focused on the agent of action or the origin of the object, 是……的 structure is more commonly used.

Japanese Verb stem + 終わる・終える (to finish doing something)

This structure is used to mean "finish doing" such as 食べ終わる、

飲み終わる。In Korean, there is a "verb stem + 기를 마치다/기가 끝나다" construction in which 기 is a nominalizer. Either the object particle 를 or the subject particle 가 attaches to the nominalizer depending on the transitivity (마치다 is a transitive verb and 끝나다 is an intransitive verb). In Chinese, the verb complement 完 is used to indicate the completion of an action.

1. 作文をやっと書き終えた。(I finished writing an essay.)
에세이 쓰기를 마침내 마쳤어요.
我写完了作文。

2. 作文がやっと書き終わった。(Writing an essay is finished.)
에세이 쓰기가 마침내 끝났어요.
作文写完了。(The subject is omitted in the sentence.)

3. コーヒーを飲み終えて、仕事に戻った。(I finished drinking coffee and returned to work.)
커피 마시기를 마치고, 직장으로 돌아갔어요.
我喝完咖啡，(然后)回去工作了。

4. 本を読み終えて、出かけました。(I finished reading a book and went out.)
책 읽기를 마치고 밖으로 나갔어요.
我看完书，(然后)出去了。

Exercise

Complete the following exchanges.

1. A: この本おもしろい？(Is this book interesting?)

B: うん。おもしろいよ。＿＿＿＿＿＿＿＿貸すよ。

(Yes. I will lend it to you when I finish reading.)

A: ありがとう。(Thanks!)

2. A: コンピューター、＿＿＿＿＿＿＿＿。消しましょうか。

(I am done using the computer. Should I turn it off?)

B: いいえ、後で使いますから、消さないで下さい。

(Please don't as I will use it later.)

A: はい。(Okay)

3. A: ごちそうさま。テレビ見てもいい？(I finished the meal. Can I watch TV now?)

B: ダメですよ。皆が＿＿＿＿＿＿＿＿待ちなさい。

(No. Wait until everyone finishes eating.)

A: は〜い。(Okay.)

4. A: レポートをもう出しましたか。(Did you turn in your report yet?)

B: いえ、さっき＿＿＿＿＿＿＿＿、今もう一度読んでいます。

(No, I finished writing it a while ago and I am reading it again.)

Activity 1

Make questions and answer about yesterday's activities:

1. A: What did you do yesterday?

B: I did my homework (cooked, ate dinner with my friend, ···).

2. A: What time did you finish your homework?

B: I finished my homework around 5 pm.

Activity 2

Make questions and answer them using the example conversation:

1. A: What is your hobby?

B: I like ______________ (cook, learn foreign languages, play computer games, etc).

A: When did you begin ______________?

B: ______________________________.

2. A: Where do you live?

B: I live in New York City.

A: When did you start living in New York City?

16

Romans/로마서/罗马书/ロ一マ人への手紙
1:16

For I am not ashamed of the gospel, because it is the power of God that brings salvation to everyone who believes: first to the Jew, then to the Gentile.

나는 복음을 부끄러워하지 않습니다. 이 복음은 유대 사람을 비롯하여 그리스 사람에게 이르기까지, 모든 믿는 사람을 구원하는 하나님의 능력입니다.

我不以福音为耻； 这福音本是 神的大能，
Wǒ bù yǐ fúyīn wéi chǐ; zhè fúyīn běn shì shén de dà néng,
要救一切相信的， 先是犹太人， 后是希腊人。
yào jiù yīqiè xiāngxìn de, xiānshi yóutàirén, hòu shì xīlà rén.

わたしは福音(ふくいん)を恥(はじ)としない。それは、ユダヤ人(じん)をはじめ、ギリシヤ人(じん)にも、すべて信(しん)じる者(もの)に、救(すくい)を得(え)させる神(かみ)の力(ちから)である。

Chinese

以…为…: to consider...as..., おもう [思う], 여기다

耻: to be ashamed of, は-じる [恥じる], 부끄러워 하다

这: this, これ, 이

本: originally, ほんらい [本来], 본래

救: to save, すく-う [救う], 구원하다

大能: power, ちから [力], 능력

相信: to believe, 信じる [しんじる], 믿다

先: firstly, まず [先ず], 먼저

犹太人: Jew, ユダヤ人, 유대인

后: later, あと [後], 나중

希腊人: Greek (Gentile in this Bible), ギリシヤ人, 그리스 사람

Japanese

恥じる: to be ashamed of, 耻 [chǐ], 부끄럽다

ユダヤ人: Jewish, 犹太人 [Yóutàirén], 유대인

はじめ: first, 先 [xiān], 처음

ギリシヤ人: Greek (Gentile in this Bible), 希腊人 [xīlàrén], 그리스 사람

すべて: entire, 都 [dōu], 모든

信じる: to believe, 相信 [xiāngxìn], 믿다

救: salvation, 救援 [jiùyuán], 구원

得: to gain, 得 [dé], 얻다

させる: to let, 使 [shǐ], ~게 하다

力: power, 能 [néng], 능력

Korean

유대 사람: Jewish, 犹太人 [Yóutàirén], ユダヤ人

비롯하다: to begin, 出于 [chūyú], はじ-める [始める]

그리스 사람: Greek (Gentile in this Bible), 希腊人 [xīlàrén], ギリシヤ人

이르다: to reach, 到 [dào], いた-る [至る·到る]

모든: entire, 都 [dōu], すべて

그리스 사람: Greek (Gentile in this Bible), 希腊人, ギリシヤ人, 믿다: to believe, 相信 [xiāngxìn], 信じる [しんじる]

구원하다: to save, 救 [jiù], すく-う [救う]

능력: power, 能 [néng], ちから [力]

Sequential order "first~, then~": 先~ 再~, ~をはじめ~も, ~을 비롯하여 ~에 이르기까지

There are a variety of ways to express sequential order in each language. Here, the expressions above indicate a set of related events, movements, or items that follow each other.

Examples

1. During this summer break, I'd like to trip around East Asia, first China then Korea and Japan.

C 今年暑假，我想去东亚旅游，先去中国，再去韩国和日本。

K 이번 여름 방학에 중국을 비롯하여 한국과 일본에 이르기까지 동아시아를 여행할 거예요.

J 今年の夏に、東アジアを旅行したい。中国をはじめ、韓国、日本へも行きたい。

A: What do you do in your free time?

C 有空的时候你会做什么？

K 시간 있을 때 뭐 해요?

J 時間があるときに何をしますか？

B: I enjoy sports. I like everything from soccer to basketball, baseball, tennis, and swimming.

C 我喜欢运动。足球，篮球，棒球，网球各种各种各样的运动，我都喜欢。

K 스포츠를 좋아해요. 축구를 비롯해서 야구, 농구, 테니스, 수영에 이르기까지 다 좋아해요.

J 私はスポーツを楽しんでいます。私はサッカーをはじめ、バスケットボール、野球、テニス、そして水泳まですべてが好きです。

Exercise

1. You will do the two activities below after you return home today. Please fill in the blanks with the sequential word.

First event: 吃饭 to eat 食事する 식사 Second Event: 看电视, to watch TV, テレビを見る, 텔레비전 시청

今天回家以后，我______吃饭，______看电视。

家に帰ったら、食事を______, テレビを見ることも______。

집에 돌아와서, 식사를 ____________, 티비 시청 ________.

2. What would you do after you return home today? Use the sequential words to create a sentence.

Korean ~어/아 하다

Emotional adjectives function either to describe the speaker's feelings or to make questions about the listener's emotions. In Korean, most of the emotional adjectives are turned into verbs by attaching -(어/아)하다 to describe a 3rd person's emotions, making the adjectives into transitive verbs.

좋다 to be good → 좋아하다 to like

배고프다 to be hungry → 배고파하다 to feel hungry

슬프다 to be sad → 슬퍼하다 to mourn

싫다 to be disagreeable → 싫어하다 to dislike

피곤하다 to be tired → 피곤해하다 to feel tired

미안하다 to be sorry → 미안해하다 to feel sorry

*밉다 to be hateful → 미워하다 to hate

*어렵다 to be difficult → 어려워하다 to feel hard, to be uncomfortable

*즐겁다 to be joyful → 즐거워하다 to enjoy

Japanese has similar ways to describe the feelings as well by adding 「がる」to certain adjectives such as さびしがる vs さびしい。 It is common to use ~ている instead of ~がる to describe someone's feelings at the current moment. Changing the 「る」in 「がる」to「り」make the adjective into a noun such as さびしがり, meaning someone who tends to feel lonely. You can add 「や」as a suffix (さびしがりや) to some of these nouns.

さびしい (lonely) →さびしがる

嫌 (disagreeable) →嫌がる

悲しい (sad) →悲しがる

怖い (scary) →怖がる

恐ろしい (scary) →恐ろしがる

暑い (hot) →暑がる

寒い (cold) →寒がる

恥ずかしい (shy) →恥ずかしがる

There are no conjugations in Chinese. Therefore, both adjectives and verbs are used to express feelings and emotions.

A: Why aren't you riding roller coasters?

K 왜 롤러 코스터를 타지 않으세요?

J ジェットコースターに乗らないの。

C 你为什么不坐过山车？

B: It's scary to ride roller coasters. Isn't it scary for you?

K 저는 롤러 코스터 타기가 무서워요. 롤러 코스터 타기가 안 무서워요?

J ジェットコースターに乗るのはこわいよ。こわくないの？

C 坐过山车很吓人。你不怕吗？

A: No, I'm not. It's exciting. But my mom has a fear of it, too.

K 안 무서워요. 재미있어요. 그런데 제 엄마도 롤러 코스터 타기를 무서워 해요.

J こわくなんかないよ。でも、お母さんはこわがってる。

C 我不怕。我觉得很有意思，但是我妈妈也怕。

Exercise

1. A: Jenny got married last weekend.

K 제니가 지난 주말에 결혼을 했어요.

C 珍妮上个星期结婚了。

J ジェニーは先週の週末結婚しましたよ。

B: I was there too. Jenny seemed really happy.

K 저도 결혼식에 갔어요. 제니가 정말 (행복하다) __________.

C 我也在。珍妮看起来很__________。

J 私も行きました。ジェニーはとても幸せそうでした。(cannot use 「がる」 here.)

2. Steve worked all night. He seemed tired.

K 스티브하고 밤새 일했어요. 스티브가 (피곤하다) __________.

C 史蒂夫一整晚都在工作。他看起来很 ________________。

J スティーブは一晩中仕事しました。とても疲れているようです。(cannot use 「がる」 here.)

3. Diane is bad at Math. She finds Math difficult.

K 다이앤이 수학을 못해요. 다이앤은 수학을 (어렵다) __________.

C 戴安数学不好。她觉得数学很 ________________。

J ダイアンは数学が苦手です。難しいみたいです。(cannot use 「がる」 here.)

Activity

Ask and answer questions about last weekend's activities with your classmates. Then describe their feelings.

17

Romans/로마서/罗马书/ローマ人への手紙
3:23

All have sinned and fall short of the glory of God.

모든 사람이 죄를 범하였습니다. 그래서 사람은 하나님의 영광에 못 미치는 처지에 놓여 있습니다.

世人都犯了罪， 亏缺了 神的荣耀。
Shìrén dōu fànle zuì, kuī quēle shén de róngyào.

すなわち、すべての人(ひと)は罪(つみ)を犯し(おか)したため、神(かみ)の栄光(えいこう)を受(う)けられなくなっている。

Chinese

世人: people, せじん [世人], 세인

都: all, すべて, 모든

犯: to commit, おか-す [犯す], 범하다

亏缺: let down, とぼし-い [乏しい], 결핍하다

荣耀: glory, えいこう [栄光], 영광

Japanese

すなわち: that is (to say), 就 [jiù], 곧

罪: sin, 罪 [zuì], 죄

犯: to commit, 犯 [fàn], 범하다

栄光: glory, 荣耀 [róngyào], 영광

受ける: to receive, 受 [shòu], 받다

Korean

모든: entire, 都 [dōu], すべて

범하다: to commit, 犯 [fàn], おか-す [犯す]

그래서: therefore, 所以 [suǒyǐ], そこで

영광: glory, 荣耀 [róngyào], えいこう [栄光]

미치다: to reach, 到 [dào], いた-る [至る·到る]

처지: position, 处境 [chǔjìng], たちば [立場]
놓이다: to be put, 放下 [fàngxià], 置かれる [おかれる]

Perfective/Resultative 了, ~ている, ~어/아 있다

In Japanese and Korean, both ~なっている and ~어/아 있다 express a result that an action has brought to completion. Chinese is known as a non-tense language; the aspect marker 了 denotes that an event has been completed in a perfective aspect. To describe the state of an object, 着 is used instead.

1. The window is open.
K 창문이 열려 있어요.
C 窗开着。
J 窓が開いている。

2. I am on top of the mountaintop. (Lit. I completed climbing up the mountaintop.)
K 산꼭대기에 올라가 있어요.
C 我爬到了山顶。
J 山に登っている。

3. The money is on the floor. (Lit. Money has fallen on the floor.)

K 돈이 바닥에 떨어져 있어요.

C 钱掉在了地上。

J お金が床に落ちている。

Exercise

1. The stores are closed on Sunday.

K 일요일에는 가게들이 (닫히다) ______________.

C 商店星期日 ______________。

J 店は日曜日は ______________。

2. The mountains are covered with snow.

K 산마다 눈으로 (덮이다) ______________.

C 山被雪 覆盖着。

J 山は雪に ______________ます。 ______________。

3. Time Square is always crowded with people.

K 타임스퀘어는 항상 사람들로 (가득하다) ______________.

C 时代广场人山人海。

J タイムズスクエアはいつも人でいっぱいです。 (〜ているis not used here)

4. The lights are turned on in my room.

K 방에 불이 (켜다) __________.

C 我房间的灯开着。

J 私の部屋の電気はついていません。

5. The sun has floated over the Atlantic Ocean.

K 대서양에 태양이 (떠오르다) __________.

C 太阳漂浮在大西洋上。

J 太陽は大西洋に浮かんでいます。

Japanese「ため(に)」reason

The clausal connective ため denotes the cause of the following event. An adjective/verb appears prior to ため and a noun to のため, which is interestingly correspondant to Korean 때문에 where a verb/adjective comes before 기 때문에 and a noun before 때문에. In Chinese, the most common conjunction to introduce a reason is 因为, which always appears at the beginning of a sentence. The other conjunction 所以 (so, therefore) is sometimes used together with 因为 to clarify the causal relationship of the two sentences.

1. Due to the rain, the picnic has been canceled.

K 오늘 비 때문에 소풍이 취소되었어요.

C 今日は雨のためピクニックは中止になりました。

J 因为下雨，野餐取消了。

2. Because I have an important test tomorrow, I cannot go out to have fun.

K 내일 중요한 시험이 있기 때문에 오늘 나가서 놀 수 없어요.

C 明日は大事な試験があるため、今日は出かけられません。

J 因为我明天有一个重要的考试，不能出去玩。

3. Because there was an earthquake, the trains stopped.

K 지진 때문에 기차가 멈췄어요.

C 地震があったため、電車が止まりました。

J 因为有地震，火车停运了。

4. You need a car since it is inconvenient around here.

K 이 근처는 불편하기 때문에 자동차가 필요해요.

C この辺は不便なため、車が必要です。

J 因为这附近不方便，你需要一辆车。

5. Because of its good quality, this product sells well.

K 이 제품은 성능이 좋기 때문에 잘 팔려요.

C この製品は性能がいいため、よく売れる。

J 因为这个产品质量好，所以卖得很好。

Exercise

1. Because I didn't eat breakfast, I had lunch early.

J 朝ごはんを食べなかったため、昼ごはんを早く食べました。

K 저는 아침을 (안 먹다) ______________, 점심을 일찍 먹었어요.

C ______ 我不吃早饭，所以早点吃午饭。

2. A: What made you come to school late?

B: I was unable to wake up early, because I went to bed late.

J A: どうして遅刻したんですか。

B: ______、早く起きれませんでした。

K A: 오늘 왜 학교에 늦게 왔어요?

B: 어제 밤 늦게 (자다) ______________, 일찍 못 일어났어요.

C A: 今天为什么上课迟到？

B: 我早上起不来，______________。

3. A: Trains stopped running due to the accident, so I came by taxi.

B: Really? That must have been terrible.

J A: ______、電車が止まって、タクシーできました。

B: そうですか。大変でしたね。

K A: 사고 때문에 기차가 멈춰서 택시로 왔어요.

B: 진짜요? 큰일이었군요.

C A: ______，所以我坐出租车来的。

B: 真的吗？太糟糕了！

4. A: Aren't you going to the office?

B: Due to the schedule change, I don't have to go today.

J A: オフィスに行かないんですか。

B: ________________、今日は行かなくてもよくなりました。

K A: 우체국에 안 가세요?

B: 일정이 바뀌었기 때문에 오늘 안 가도 돼요.

C A: 你不去办公室吗？

B: ________________, 我今天不用去。

Activity

Interview your partner with such questions as where they want to live or their future goals, and follow up with 'why' questions.

18

Romans/로마서/罗马书/ローマ人への手紙
5:8

But God demonstrates his own love for us in this: While we were still sinners, Christ died for us.

그러나 우리가 아직 죄인이었을 때에, 그리스도께서 우리를 위하여 죽으셨습니다. 이리하여 하나님께서는 우리들에 대한 자기의 사랑을 실증하셨습니다.

惟有基督在我们还作罪人的时候为我们死，
Wéiyǒu jīdū zài wǒmen hái zuò zuìrén de shíhòu wèi wǒmen sǐ,
神的爱就在此向我们显明了。
shén de ài jiù zài cǐ xiàng wǒmen xiǎnmíng liǎo.

しかし、まだ罪人(ざいにん)であった時(とき)、わたしたちのためにキリストが死(し)んで下(くだ)さったことによって、神(かみ)はわたしたちに対(たい)する愛(あい)を示(しめ)されたのである。

Chinese

惟: only, ひとえに [偏に], 오직

罪人: sinner, ざいにん [罪人], 죄인

还: still, まだ, 아직

为: for, ために, 위하여

向: toward, たい-する [対する], ~에 대한

显明: to reveal, manifest, めいはく [明白], 명백하다

Japanese

しかし: however, 却 [què], 그러나

まだ: still, 还 [hái], 아직

罪人: sinner, 罪人 [zuìrén], 죄인

時: time, 时候 [shí·hou], 때

死ぬ: to die, 死 [sǐ], 죽다

下さる: to give (honorific), 赐 [cì], 주시다

対する: to face, 对 [duì], 대하다

示す: to show, 展示 [zhǎnshì], 보이다

Korean

그러나: however, 却 [què], しかし

아직: still, 还 [hái], まだ

죄인: sinner, 罪人 [zuìrén], ざいにん [罪人]

되다: to become, 作 [zuò], なる

이리하여: consequently, 由此 [yóucǐ], こうして

에 대한: towards, 对 [duì], たい-する [対する]

실증하다: to demonstrate, 实证 [shízhèng], じっしょうする [実証する]

Simultaneous Situation

~的时候，~時，and ~을 때에 "When" or "While"

These 时候， 時，and 때 refer to the time of a specific action or event. To describe a situation that an action or state takes place, the situations are followed by ~的时候，~時，and ~을 때에. They cannot be used when the relationship between the situations are sequential.

For Japanese, refer to L 13. For Korean, in the case where the situation completed, the past marker 았/었 occurs in the form of 았을 때에/었을 때에. However, as there are no tense conjugations in Chinese, no past tense is used in the ……的时候 structure.

Examples

1. While studying, I listen to music.

- **K** 공부할 때 음악을 들어요.
- **C** 我学习的时候听音乐。
- **J** 勉強している時、音楽を聴きます。

2. When I was young, I grew up in Japan.

- **K** 어렸을 때, 일본에서 자랐어요.
- **C** 我小时候在日本长大。
- **J** 小さい時、日本で育ちました。

Exercise

Fill in the blank using the word bank below and make conversation with your classmates.

1. When you are free, what do you do? [to have time, to eat alone,…]

- **K** ______때 뭐 하세요? [시간이 있다, 혼자 밥 먹다, …]
- **C** ______的时候，你做什么？[有空，自己吃饭]
- **J** ______時、何がしたいですか。

2. When you have nothing to do, who do you call? [to be bored, to want to hang out,…]

K ______ 때 누구한테 전화해요? [심심하다, 놀고 싶다, …]

C ______ 的时候，你给谁打电话？[无聊，想出去玩]

J ______ 時、誰に電話をしますか。

3. While you were in your hometown, where did you live? [to have been in your hometown, to have been attending school,…]

K ______ 때 어디서 살았어요? [고향에 있었다, 대학교에 다녔다, …]

C ______ 的时候，你住在哪里？[在老家，上学]

J ______ 時、どこに住んでいましたか。

4. When your stomach hurts, what do you do? [to hurt, to be scared, to doze off, …]

K ______ 때 어떻게 해요? [배가 아프다, 무섭다, 졸리다, …]

C ______ 的时候，你做什么？[伤心，害怕，想睡觉]

J ______ 時、何をしますか。

5. Who do you go shopping with? [to go shopping, to eat out,…]

K ______ 때 누구하고 같이 가세요? [쇼핑하러 가다, 식당에 밥 먹으러 가다, …]

C ______ 的时候，你跟谁去？[买东西]

J ____ 時、誰と一緒に行きますか。

Chinese Word Order

1. Topic + subject + predicate: 咖啡我没喝过。

2. Subject + verb + indirect object + direct object: 我给你一本书。

3. Subject + Time + Place + predicate: 我每天在家吃饭。

4. Subject + prepositional phrase + verb + object: 他跟他的奴朋友吃晚饭。

19

Romans/로마서/罗马书/ローマ人への手紙
8:1, 2

Therefore, there is now no condemnation for those who are in Christ Jesus, 2 because through Christ Jesus the law of the Spirit who gives life has set you[a] free from the law of sin and death.

그러므로 그리스도 예수 안에 있는 사람들은 정죄를 받지 않습니다. 그것은, 그리스도 예수 안에서 생명을 누리게 하는 성령의 법이 당신을 죄와 죽음의 법에서 해방하여 주었기 때문입니다.

如今，那些在基督耶稣里的就不定罪了。
Rújīn, nàxiē zài jīdū yēsū lǐ de jiù bù dìngzuìle.
因为赐生命圣灵的律，在基督耶 稣里释放了我，
Yīnwèi cì shēngmìng shènglíng de lǜ, zài jīdū yē sū lǐ shìfàngle wǒ,
使我脱离罪和死的律了。
shǐ wǒ tuōlí zuì hé sǐ de lǜle.

こういうわけで、今(いま)やキリスト・イエスにある者(もの)は罪(つみ)に定(さだ)められることがない。なぜなら、キリスト・イエスにあるいのちの御霊(ごりょう)の法則(ほうそく)は、罪(つみ)と死(し)との法則(ほうそく)からあなたを解放(かいほう)したからである。

Chinese

如今: today, いま, 지금

那些: those, それら, 그들/그것들

里: inside, うら [裏] , 안에

定罪: to convict, せ-める [責める], 정죄하다

因为: because, なぜなら, 왜냐하면

赐: to give, 与える [あたえる], 주다

生命: life, いのち, 생명

圣灵: Holy Spirit, ごりょう [御霊], 성령

律: law, ほうそく [法則], 법

释放: to set free, かいほう [解放], 해방하다

脱离: to get away from, だっ-する [脱する], 벗어나다

和: and, と, 와/과

Japanese

こういうわけで: therefore, 由此 [yóucǐ], 이로써

今や: now, 如今 [rújīn], 지금이야말로

ある: to exist, 有 [yǒu], 있다

罪: sin, 罪 [zuì], 죄

定める: to determine, 定 [dìng], 정하다

なぜなら: because, 因为 [yīn · wèi], 왜냐하면

いのち: life, 生命 [shēngmìng], 생명

御霊: Holy Spirit, 圣灵 [shènglíng], 성령

法則: law, 律 [lǜ], 법

から: from, 从 [cóng], 으로부터

解放: to liberate, 释放 [shìfàng], 해방하다

Korean

그러므로: therefore, 所以 [suǒyǐ], だから

있다: to be/exist, 有 [yǒu], ある

정죄: judgement, 判断 [pànduàn], はんだん [判断]

받다: to receive, 受 [shòu], 受ける [うける]

생명: life, 生命 [shēngmìng], いのち

누리다: to enjoy, 享受 [xiǎngshòu], う-ける [受ける]

법: law, 律 [lǜ], ほうそく [法則]

해방하다: to liberate, 释放 [shìfàng], かいほう [解放]

Positions 在~里，~にある，~안에 있다

This structure is used to indicate the existence of objects and the locational entity. To show where an object is in relation to another object, you can use positional words to further specify the location of an entity such as:

영어	on	under	front	back	next to	right	left	inside	outside
중국어	上(面)	下(面)	前(面)	后(面)	旁边	右边	左边	里(面)	外(面)
일본어	上 (うえ)	下 (した)	前 (まえ)	後ろ (うしろ)	隣 (となり)	右 (みぎ)	左 (ひだり)	中 (なか)	外 (そと)
한글	위	아래	앞	뒤	옆	오른쪽	왼쪽	안	밖

Note the word order of the location of the entity, position noun, and position marker. In Chinese, the preposition word 在 precedes location words whereas in both Japanese and Korean, the postposition word に and 에 follow the location words respectively.

Chinese: position marker 在+locational entity+positional word (ex: 在包里)

Japanese: locational entity+positional noun+position marker に (ex: カバン中に)

Korean: locational entity+positional noun+position marker 에 (ex: 가방 안에)

A: 你的手机在包里吗？

B: 在位子上。

A: 携帯電話はカバンの中にありますか。

B: いすの上にあります。

A: 휴대폰이 가방 안에 있어요?

B: 의자 위에 있어요.

Activity

Describe the position of objects around you.

Possibility/Impossibility in Japanese

「verb present tense + ことがある/ことがない」

こと means things, and ある means 'to exist'. The combination of the construction above indicates "there are times in which what is described by the verb happens/never happens". This is quite similar to Korean construction 'verb stem + present tense modifier 는 + 경우가 있다/없다'. 경우 (occasion) can be replaced with 일 (event), 수 (occasion), and 때 (time).

1. I usually drink coffee but there are times I drink tea.

J たいていコーヒーを飲みますが、お茶を飲むこともあります。

K 대체로 커피를 마시지만 차를 마시는 경우가 있어요.

C 我常常喝咖啡，但也有喝茶的时候。

2. There are times I don't have breakfast.

J 朝ご飯を食べないことがあります。

K 아침을 먹지 않는 경우가 있어요.

C 我有不吃早饭的时候。

3. Lee is diligent and there is never a time he comes to class late.

J リーさんはまじめで授業に遅れることはありません。

K 이 선생은 부지런해서 수업에 늦는 경우가 없어요.

C 李很勤奋，上课从来不迟到。

Exercise

Fill in the blanks.

1. Sometimes I commute to work by walking.

(걸어서 출근하다) ______________________.

2. My friend never drinks alcohol when he needs to drive his car.

내 친구는 차를 운전할 때, (술을 마시다) ______________.

3. There are times I feel dizzy when I get up in the morning.

아침에 일어 날 때, (머리가 어지럽다) ______________.

4. I sometimes forget people's names these days.

요즘들어 사람의 이름을 (잊어버리다) ______________.

20

Romans/로마서/罗马书/ローマ人への手紙

8:9

You, however, are not in the realm of the flesh but are in the realm of the Spirit, if indeed the Spirit of God lives in you. And if anyone does not have the Spirit of Christ, they do not belong to Christ.

그러나 하나님의 영이 여러분 안에 살아 계시면, 여러분은 육신 안에 있지 않고, 성령 안에 있습니다. 누구든지 그리스도의 영이 없으면, 그리스도의 사람이 아닙니다.

如果 神的灵住在你们心里，你们就不属肉体，
Rúguǒ shén de líng zhù zài nǐmen xīnlǐ, nǐmen jiù bù shǔ ròutǐ,
乃属圣灵了。人若没有基 督的灵，就不是属基督的。
nǎi shǔ shènglíngle. Rén ruò méiyǒu jī dū de líng, jiù bùshì shǔ jīdū de.

しかし、神(かみ)の御霊(ごりょう)があなたがたの内(うち)に宿(やど)っているなら、あなたがたは肉(にく)におるのではなく、霊(れい)におるのである。もし、キリストの霊(れい)を持た(もた)ない人(ひと)がいるなら、その人(ひと)はキリストのものではない。

Chinese

如果: if, なら, (으)면

灵: Spirit, たましい [魂·霊], 영

住: to live, やど-る [宿る], 살다

你们: you (plural), あなたがた, 여러분

属: to belong to, ぞく-する [属する], 속하다

肉体: flesh, にく [肉], 육신

若: if, もし, 혹시

没有: to not have, ~ない, ~이/가 없다

Japanese

しかし: however, 却 [què], 그러나

肉: flesh, 肉体 [ròutǐ], 육체

宿る: to live, 住 [zhù], 살다

お-る: to be, 在 [zài], 있다

もし: if, 若 [ruò], 만약

持つ: to hold, 持 [chí], 가지다

いる: to be, 在 [zài], 있다

もの: thing/person, ~的, 것/사람

Korean

그러나: however, 却 [què], しかし

여러분: you (plural, honorific), 您们 [nín · men], 皆さん [みなさん]

안: inside, 内, うち

누구든지: whoever, 无论是谁, だれしも [誰しも]

없다: to not have, 没有 [méi · yǒu], ~ない

아니다: to not be, 不是 [bú · shi], …で(は)ない

Japanese Supposition なら vs たら

Another form of the conditional expression is "なら". Unlike "たら", "なら" requires some context and is only used under specific circumstances. The general meaning is something like "if it is indeed the case" or "provided that...". This corresponds to Korean '다면', before which the plain style of verb or adjective form is used. In Chinese, the conjunctions 如果 and 要是 are used at the beginning of the first clause, with 就 sometimes used in the second clause to indicate the result of the hypothetical situation.

Verb /i-adjective plain form + なら

食べるなら・食べないなら・食べたなら・食べなかったなら

おいしいなら・おいしくないなら・おいしかったなら・おいしくなかったなら

Noun/ na-adjective + なら

学生なら・学生じゃないなら・学生だったなら・学生じゃなかったなら

ひまなら・ひまじゃないなら・ひまだったなら・ひまじゃなかったなら

1. A: Would you like to go to the party?

J 中山：パーティーに行きませんか。

K 파티에 가지 않을래요?

C 你想去派对吗？

B: If you are going, I will go too.

J 内田：中山さんが行くなら、私も行きます。

K 나카야마 씨가 간다면 저도 가겠어요.

C 要是你去，我就去。

2. A: Is Tanaka-san going to leave the company? Nakayama-san has said so.

J 田中さん、会社やめるんですか。中山さんが言っていました。

K 다나카 씨, 회사를 그만두실 건가요? 나카야마 씨가 그렇게 말했어요.

C 田中先生要离开公司了吗，中山先生说的。

B: If Nakayama-san says so, it may be true.

J 中山さんが言うなら、本当かもしれないね。

K 나카야마 씨가 그렇게 말한다면, 정말일지도 모르겠네요.

C 要是中山先生这么说，那就是真的。

3. A: This bag is nice. I want it.

J このカバンいいな。ほしいな。

K 이 가방이 좋군요. 갖고 싶네요.

C 这个包很漂亮，我想要。

B: If you want it, why don't you buy it?

J ほしいなら買ったらどう。

K 갖고 싶다면 사시지요.

C 要是你想要，为什么不买呢？

4. A: Where is the book we borrowed from Uchida-san?

J 内田さんから借りている本はどこでしょうか。

K 우치다 씨한테서 빌린 책이 어디에 있어요?

C 我们跟内田先生借的书在哪里？

B: Oh, if in that case you're speaking of that book, it's on Yamanaka-san's desk.

J あ、その本なら、今山中さんのつくえの上にありますよ。

K 아, 그 책이라면 지금 야마나카 씨의 책상 위에 있어요.

C 噢，要是你说的是那本书，那再山中先生的桌子上。

■ Fill in the blanks.

1. A: May I watch TV?

J テレビを見てもいい。

K 텔레비전을 봐도 돼요?

C 我可以看电视吗？

B: Did you finish your homework? if ···, you may.

J 宿題終わったの。 ________________________見てもいいよ。

K 숙제를 끝냈다면 봐도 돼요.

C 你做完功课了吗？ ________________________, 就可以。

2. A: Can I take a break?

J ちょっと休んでもいいですか。

K 좀 쉬어도 돼요?

C 我可以休息吗？

B: You may if ···

J ____________________いいですよ。

K ________________________, 좋습니다.

C ________________________就可以。

3. A: I will go shopping.

J ちょっと買い物に行ってきます。

K 쇼핑 좀 하고 올게요.

C 我去买东西了。

B: If···, please buy some milk.

J ________________ ミルクを買ってきてください。

K ________________ 우유 좀 사다 주세요.

C ________________, 请买一些牛奶。

Korean Indefinite pronouns 누구든지

Interrogative-indefinite pronouns such as 누구 'who, someone', 무엇 'what, something', 어디 'where, somewhere', 언제 'when, some time', 얼마 'how much, some amount', and the compoundings 어느 사람/곳/때/것 'who/where/when/what' become emphatic with 든지.

Similarly in Japanese, Interrogative + か means "someone", "someday", "somewhere", etc,, and Interrogative + でも means "anyone", "anyday", "anywhere", etc. In addition, Interrogative + も + affirmative ending means "everyone", "everyday", and "everywhere", and so on.

In Chinese, the word for "any", "任何(rènhé)", is used before a noun such as things, people, places and time to express the "anything, anyonc, anywhere and anytime".

1. Any student can get a 20% discount on admission tickets.

K 학생은 누구든지 입장권을 20% 할인 받을 수 있어요.

J 学生はだれでも入場券が２割安くなる。

C 任何学生买门票都可以打八折。

2. I eat everything except meat.

K 저는 고기만 빼고 무엇이든지 잘 먹어요.

J 肉以外は何でも食べます。

C 我除了肉，任何食物都吃。

3. Feel free to call me if you need any help.

K 도움이 필요하면 언제든지 전화하세요.

J 何かあったらいつでも電話してください。

C 要是你需要任何帮助，请给我打电话。

4. In Manhattan it is convenient to take the subway so you can go anywhere.

K 맨하탄은 지하철이 편해서 어디든지 갈 수 있어요.

J マンハッタンは地下鉄でどこへでも行けるので便利です。

C 曼哈顿坐地铁很方便，去任何地方都可以。

Exercise

1. There are many cars everywhere during the holidays. It's convenient to just stay at home.

K 연휴 때는 ________________ 차가 많아요. 그냥 집에 있는 게 편해요.

J 休みの間は ________________。うちにいる方が楽です。

C 过节的时候 ________________。待在家最方便了。

2. I'll be home tomorrow. You can come anytime.

K 내일 집에 있을 테니까 ________________ 와도 돼요.

J 明日はうちにいます。いつでも来てください。(いつ来てもいいです。)

C 我明天回家，你 ________________ 都可以来。

3. I like any kind of exercise.

K 저는 운동은 ________________ 좋아해요.

J 運動は何でも好きです。(どんな運動でも好きです。)

C ________________ 我都喜欢。

4. Tomorrow is my birthday. Anyone can come to the party.

K 내일 제 생일이에요. 파티에 ________________ 올 수 있어요.

J 明日は私の誕生日です。パーティーにはだれでも来られます。(パーティーにはだれが来てもいいです。)

C 明天是我的生日。 ____________________ 都可以来我的派对。

Activity

Make conversations that would take place in these situations using the grammar structures from the chapter.

1. Favorite food: proposal for having lunch or dinner together

2. Favorite sports: proposal for hosting a joint sports activity

21

Romans/로마서/罗马书/ローマ人への手紙
8:15

The Spirit you received does not make you slaves, so that you live in fear again; rather, the Spirit you received brought about your adoption to sonship. And by him we cry, "Abba, Father."

여러분은 또다시 두려움에 빠뜨리는 종살이의 영을 받은 것이 아니라, 자녀로 삼으시는 영을 받았습니다. 그래서 우리는 그 영으로 하나님을 "아빠, 아버지"라고 부릅니다.

你们所受的， 不是奴仆的心， 仍旧害怕；所受的，
Nǐmen suǒ shòu de, bùshì núpú de xīn, réngjiù hàipà; suǒ shòu de,
乃是儿子的心， 因此我 们呼叫：「阿爸! 父!」
nǎi shì érzi de xīn, yīncǐ wǒ men hūjiào: `Ā bà! Fù!'

あなたがたは再(ふたた)び恐(おそ)れをいだかせる奴隷(どれい)の霊(れい)を受け(うけ)たのではなく、子(こ)たる身分(みぶん)を授(さず)ける霊(れい)を受(う)けたのである。その霊(れい)によって、わたしたちは「アバ、父(ちち)よ」と呼(よ)ぶのである。

Chinese

受: to receive, 受ける [うける], 받다

不是: to not be, …で(は)ない, 아니다

奴仆: slave, どれい [奴隷], 종

旧: old, きゅう [旧], 옛날의

害怕: fear, おそれ [恐れ], 두려움

儿子: child, こども [子ども·子供], 자녀

因此: therefore, ここにおいて, 이로써

我们: we, わたしたち, 우리

呼叫: to cry, よ-ぶ [呼ぶ], 부르다

Japanese

再び: again, 再次 [zàicì], 또다시

恐れ: fear, 恐惧 [kǒngjù], 두려움

いだ-く [懐く]: to bear, 怀抱 [huáibào], 품다

奴隷: slave, 奴仆 [núpú], 종

身分: status, 身份 [shēn fen], 신분

授ける: to give, 给与 [gěiyǔ], 주다

受ける: to receive, 受 [shòu], 받다

によって: by, 依 [yī], ...에 의해

呼ぶ: to call, 呼叫 [hūjiào], 외치다

Korean

또다시: again, 再次 [zàicì], ふたたび [再び]

두려움: fear, 恐惧 [kǒngjù], おそれ [恐れ]

빠뜨리다: to drop, 把[bǎ]…抛进 [pāojìn], 落とす [おとす]

받다: to receive, 受 [shòu], 受ける [うける]

삼다: to make, 当作 [dàngzuò], …にする

Korean Instrument Marker ~(으)로 by means of

The Korean particle ~(으)로 is surprisingly polysemous, marking direction in the sense of 'for, to', instrument in the sense of 'with, by', and function in the sense of 'as, in terms of'. Here, the instrument marking aspect will be introduced first and the others will be commented on later.

The Japanese particle で can be used to indicate means, method, or instruments. It translates to "by", "with", "in," "by means of", etc.

In Chinese, "by means of" is generally translated to preposition words such as "用(yòng)、依靠(yīkào)、凭借(píngjiè)、通过(tōngguò)" to express the meaning of "with the help or agency of". 用 literally means "to use", and so it is commonly used to express the utilization of physical instruments to achieve the purpose of the action. “依靠、凭借、通过” are generally used to express abstract meanings. However, these words are not as versatile as their Korean counterpart “(으)로” and cannot be used in the sense of “for, to”, and “as, in terms of.”

1. We call God “Father” by the Spirit.

- **K** 우리는 영으로 하나님을 아버지라고 부릅니다.
- **C** 我们借着圣灵称神为“父”。
- **J** 私たちは霊で神をお父さんと呼びます。

2. Houses made of wood are easy to burn.

- **K** 나무로 지은 집은 불에 타기 쉬워요.
- **C** 用木头做的房子很容易着火。
- **J** 木で造った家は燃えやすいです。

3. Since 2020, people have suffered a lot from coronavirus.

- **K** 2020년부터 코로나 바이러스로 사람들이 고생을 많이 했어요.
- **C** 2020年以来，人们深受新冠病毒之苦。
- **J** 2020年からコロナウイルスで人が苦労をたくさんしました。

Exercise

1. Linda is doing her homework on her laptop.

K 린다가 ________________ 숙제를 하고 있어요.

C 琳达 ________________________________ 做功课。

J リンダが ____________________________ 宿題をしています。

2. Jane is watching a movie on YouTube.

K 제인이 ________________ 영화를 보고 있어요.

C 简 ________________________________ 看电影。

J ジェーンが ___________________________ 映画を見ています。

3. Steve is taking a picture with a camera.

K 스티브가 ________________ 사진을 찍어요.

C 史蒂夫 ________________________________ 拍照。

J スティーブが ___________________________ 写真を撮ります。

4. Mom is cutting meat with a knife.

K 엄마가 ________________ 고기를 썰어요.

C 妈妈 ________________________________ 切肉。

J お母さんが ____________________________ 肉を切ります。

Activity

Find out how classmates get to school using different modes of transportation.

Japanese causative construction

Causative construction roughly means "A causes B to perform some action or event". The Japanese causative is realized through verb conjugation, which also applies to Korean. However, Korean has two types of causative constructions; one is the short form, created by adding causative suffixes such as 이, 히, 리, 기 to the verb stem. The other is the long form, adding phrasal causative 게 하다 after a predicate. Compare the basic form with its causative counterparts in both languages. In Chinese, the causative verb 让 (ràng) is adopted to express a similar meaning. For example, the structure "A让B+adjective/verb" means "A makes B adjective or A makes B do something."

- いだく→いだかせる

るverbs take out the 「る」 and change to させる

食べる→食べさせる 먹다 → 먹이다/먹게 하다

見る →見させる 보다 → 보이다/보게 하다

● うverbs change the last sound [u] to [a] and addせる

書く→書かせる 쓰다 → 쓰게 하다

読む→読ませる 읽다 → 읽게 하다

使う→使わせる 시키다 → 시키게 하다

● Irregular する→させる 하다 → 하게 하다

来る→来させる 오다 → 오게 하다

1. Parents make their children do their homework.

J 親は子供に宿題をさせる。

K 부모님께서 아이들에게 숙제를 하게 해요.

C 父母让孩子做功课。

2. The store manager made the clerks work until late.

J 店長は店員に遅くまで働かせた。

K 점장님께서 점원들에게 늦게까지 일을 하게 했어요.

C 店经理让员工加班。

Activities

Answer the questions:

1. If you become a parent, what will you make/let your child do?

J もし親になったら子供に何をさせますか。

K 여러분이 부모가 되면 아이들에게 무엇을 하게 할 거예요?

C 要是你做了父母，你会让孩子做什么？

2. If you were a boss, what would you make/let your subordinates do?

J もし上司だったら部下に何をさせますか。

K 여러분이 사장이라면 직원들에게 어떻게 무엇을 하게 할 거예요?

C 要是你是老板，你会让下属做什么？

22

Romans/로마서/罗马书/ローマ人への手紙
10:9,10

If you declare with your mouth, "Jesus is Lord," and believe in your heart that God raised him from the dead, you will be saved. For it is with your heart that you believe and are justified, and it is with your mouth that you profess your faith and are saved.

당신이 만일 예수는 주님이라고 입으로 고백하고, 하나님께서 그를 죽은 사람들 가운데서 살리신 것을 마음으로 믿으면 구원을 얻을 것입니다. 사람은 마음으로 믿어서 의에 이르고, 입으로 고백해서 구원에 이르게 됩니다.

你若口里认耶稣为主， 心里信 神叫他从死里复活，
Nǐ ruò kǒu lǐ rèn yēsū wéi zhǔ, xīnlǐ xìn shén jiào tā cóng sǐ lǐ fùhuó,
就必得救。 因为，人 心里相信就可以称义，
jiù bì děi jiù. Yīnwèi, rén xīnlǐ xiāngxìn jiù kěyǐ chēng yì,
口里承认就可以得救。
kǒu lǐ chéngrèn jiù kěyǐ déjiù.

すなわち、自分(じぶん)の口(くち)で、イエスは主であると告白(こくはく)し、自分(じぶん)の心(こころ)で、神(かみ)が死人(しにん)の中(なか)からイエスをよみがえらせたと信じる(しんじる)なら、あなたは救わ(すくわ)れる。なぜなら、人(ひと)は心(こころ)に信じ(しんじ)て義(ぎ)とされ、口(くち)で告白(こくはく)して救(すく)われるからである。

Chinese

若: if, もし [若し], 만약/만일

口: mouth, くち [口], 입

里: inside, うち [内], 속

认: to admit, みと-める [認める], 인정하다

信: to believe, 信じる [しんじる], 믿다

叫: to make, させる, ...하게 하다

从: from, ~から, ~에서

复活: to raise (from the dead), ふっかつする [復活する], 부활하다

救: salvation, きゅうえん [救援], 구원

相信: to believe, 信じる [しんじる], 믿다

义: righteousness, ぎ [義], 의

承认: to admit, approve, しょうにんする [承認する], 승인하다

Japanese

すなわち: that is, 也就是说 [yě jiù · shi shuō], 곧

口: mouth, 口 [kǒu], 입

こくはくする [告白する]: to confess, 告白 [gàobái], 고백하다

心: heart, 心 [xīn], 마음

中: among, 中间 [zhōngjiān], 중/가운데

よみがえる: to revive, 复活 [fùhuó], 소생하다

信じる: to believe, 相信 [xiāngxìn], 믿다

すく-う [救う]: to save, 救 [jiù], 구원하다

なぜなら: because, 因为 [yīn wèi], 왜냐하면

Korean

당신: you (written, honorific), 你 [nǐ], あなた [貴方·貴下]

가운데서: among, 中间 [zhōngjiān], なか [中]

믿다: to believe, 相信 [xiāngxìn], 信じる [しんじる]

이르다: to reach, 到达 [dàodá], いた-る [至る·到る]

The Chinese adverb 就 (jiù) just, then

In Lesson 20, we briefly mentioned the use of 就 in the conditional expression 要是…就… (if...then...). However, 就 is also used to indicate the causal relationship between two clauses. The first clause introduces the fact, while the second half including 就 is generally a related suggestion.

1. (Since) you don't want to eat, then don't eat.

C 你不想吃饭，就别吃了。

K 밥이 먹고 싶지 않으면, 먹지 마세요.

J ご飯が食べたいなら、食べないでください。

2. (Since) you want to study in China, then start studying Chinese as early as possible.

C 你想去中国留学，就早点开始学中文吧。

K 중국에 유학 가고 싶으면, 가능한 일찍 중국어 공부를 시작하세요.

J 中国に留学したいなら、早くから中国語を学び始めましょう。

3. (Since) your child is doing well in school, then try to apply for the best colleges.

C 你的孩子成绩那么好，就应该去试试考最好的大学。

K 아이가 그렇게 공부를 잘 하면, 좋은 대학에 지원해 보세요.

J 子供がそう勉強を上手にしたら、良い大学に応援してみてください。

4. (Since) it's raining, then let's not go out today.

C 下雨了，我们今天就不出门了吧。

K 비가 오니까 오늘은 나가지 맙시다.

J 雨が降っているので、今日は出かけません。

Exercises

Give your partner a suggestion based on the fact introduced in the first clause:

1. You like this piece of clothing so much, …

C 你那么喜欢这件衣服, ____________________。

K 이 옷을 좋아하면, ____________________.

J この服が好きなら、____________________。

2. Since no one is interested in playing ball, …

C 大家都没有兴趣去打球, ____________________。

K 아무도 공놀이에 관심이 없으면, ____________________.

J 誰もボール遊びに興味がなければ、____________________。

3. Since you didn't do well on this exam,…

C 你这次考试考得不太好, ____________________。

K 이번 시험을 잘 못 봤으면, ____________________.

J 今回の試験がうまくいかなかったら、____________________。

4. Since you broke up with your boyfriend already, …

C 你跟男朋友已经分手了, ____________________。

K 남자 친구하고 헤어졌으면, ____________________.

J 彼氏と別れたら、____________________。

5. Since you said you are his best friend, …

C 你说你他最好的朋友, ____________________。

K 가장 친한 친구라면, ____________________.

J 親友なら、____________________。

Indirect Quotation markers

Japanese ~と，Korean ~(이)라고/~다고

Quotation is generally used to express a clause that is reported, heard, spoken, written, suggested, thought, or believed by the speaker or another party . There are two methods of quotation: a direct quotation that reports the exact words spoken, and an indirect quotation that reports only the content.

The Korean ~(이)라고 occurs after a noun, and ~다고 occurs after a verb/adjective for statement sentences. (~냐고 is used for questions, ~(으)라고 for commands, and ~자고 for suggestions). For the quoted clause ending, the formality level that would occur in direct quotation must be neutralized.

The Japanese particle と is used to quote what was said or written, and followed by verbs such as "言います, "聞きます", "書きます". Like Korean, there are two types of quotations in Japanese: direct and indirect. In a direct quotation, the end of the quoted sentence can be either long or short form and have a quotation marker 「　」. Indirect quotations end in the short form.

Yamamoto said that s/he has a test next week.

山本さんは「来週試験があります」と言いました。

山本さんは来週試験があると言いました。

In Chinese, indirect quotation is similar to the English structure, e.g., “She said”, “the teacher told me”, etc. Sometimes a comma is used before the indirect quotation, but it is not necessary if the quoted sentence or phrase is short.

1. Mom told me she would see a doctor tomorrow.

K 엄마가 내일 의사를 만나러 간다고 말했어요.

C 我妈妈告诉我，明天她要去看医生。

J 母は明日病院に行くと言った。

2. The teacher asked us if we would be available tomorrow.

K 선생님이 내일 시간이 있냐고 물으셨어요.

C 老师问我们明天有没有空。

J 先生は明日あいているかどうか聞いた。

3. My brother texted me to come early.

K 형이 집에 일찍 오라고 문자했어요.

C 我哥哥发短信给我，让我早点来。

J 兄は早く来てとテキストしてきた。

4. My friend suggested that we go to the concert.

K 친구가 주말에 콘서트에 가자고 했어요.

C 我的朋友建议我们去听音乐会。

J 友達はコンサートにいかないかと言った。

5. I thought that New York was the best city to live in when I was in highschool.

K 저는 고등학교 때 가장 살고 싶은 도시가 뉴욕이라고 생각했어요.

C 我高中的时候觉得纽约是最适合生活的城市。

J 高校の時、ニューヨークは一番いい町だと思った。

Exercise

Change the direct quotation into an indirect quotation.

"오늘 날씨가 아주 맑아서 등산을 가요."

(Today the weather is good, so I will go to hiking.)

→ 오늘 날씨가 아주 맑아서 등산을 간다고 말했어요.

1. "제일 여행하고 싶은 곳은 하와이예요."

(Hawaii is my favorite place to travel.)

→

2. "주말에 뭐 하고 싶어요?"

(What do you want to do this weekend?)

→

3. “이쪽으로 오세요.”

(Come this way, please.)

→

4. “내일 10시에 레빈언어센타에서 만나요.”

(Let's meet at Levine Language Center at 10 tomorrow.)

→

Activity

1. Prepare a catalog/advertisement/newspaper and report the content to the classroom using indirect quotations.

2. Introduce the content of your favorite movie you have seen recently.

23

Romans/로마서/罗马书/ローマ人への手紙
11:36

For from him and through him and for him are all things. To him be the glory forever! Amen.

만물이 그에게서 나고, 그로 말미암아 있고, 그를 위하여 있습니다. 그에게 영광이 세세에 있기를 빕니다. 아멘.

因为万有都是本于他，倚靠他，归于他。
Yīnwèi wàn yǒu dōu shì běn yú tā, yǐkào tā, guīyú tā.
愿荣耀归给他，直到永远。阿们！
Yuàn róngyào guī gěi tā, zhídào yǒngyuǎn. Āmen!

万物(ばんぶつ)は、神からいで、神によって成(な)り、神に帰(き)するのである。栄光(えいこう)がとこしえに神にあるように、アァメン。

Chinese

万有: all things, ばんぶつ [万物], 만물

本: original, ほん [本], 근본의

于: from, から, 에게서

倚靠: to depend, よる, 말미암다

归: to attribute to, き-する [帰する], 귀결되다

愿: to wish, ねが-う [願う], 원하다

荣耀: glory, えいこう [栄光], 영광

直到: till, まで, 까지

永远: forever, とこしえ, 영원히

Japanese

万物: all things, 万有 [wànyǒu], 만물

から: from, 于 [yú], 에서

よる [因る]: to arise, 倚靠 [yǐkào], 말미암다

成る: to achieve, 成 [chéng], 완성되다

帰する: to attribute, 归于 [guīyú], 귀결되다

栄光: glory, 荣耀 [róngyào], 영광

とこしえ: forever, 永远 [yǒngyuǎn], 영원히

Korean

에게서: from, 于 [yú], から

나다: to come out, 出 [chū], は-える [生える]

말미암다: to arise, 倚靠 [yǐkào], よる [因る]

위하여: for, 为 [wèi], ために

영원히 : forever, 永远 [yǒngyuǎn], とこしえ

빌다: to wish, 愿 [yuàn], ねが-う [願う]

Expressing a wish or hope

There are many ways to express the speaker's wishes depending on the context. What kind of wish are you expressing? Are you speaking to a superior or a friend? Each determines a different manner by which you would express "to wish" or "to hope".

In spoken Chinese, 希望 (hope) or 祝 (wish) are the most commonly used verbs in this situation. In written/formal Chinese, 愿(wish) is sometimes used in place of 祝. **They translate to きぼうする[希望する], ねが-う [願う] in Japanese, and** 바라다, 원하다 in Korean. 바라다 and 원하다 take only conjugated verbs or adjectives. For Korean, the preceding verbs or adjectives take ~기를 (verb/adjective stem+기를) in which 기 is nominalizer and 를 is the object particle before 바라다, 원하다. It is possible to use the conditional ~으면 after the verb/adjective with 좋겠다 'to be great' in order to express a wish or hope in a similar manner.

먹다 → 먹기를 바라다
먹지 않다 → 먹지 않기를 바라다

덥다 → 더우면 좋겠다
덥지 않다 → 덥지 않으면 좋겠다

For Japanese, the ～ように（verb + ように）construction is used.

食べるように・するように
食べないように・しないように
食べますように・しますように
食べませんように・しませんように

願いがかないますように。 꿈이 실현되기를 바랍니다.
願いがかなったらいい・嬉しい。꿈이 실현되면 좋겠습니다/기쁘겠습니다.
願いがかなうように、神にお祈りした。꿈이 실현되도록 하나님께 기도했어요.
成績がよくなるように、勉強の仕方を変えた。성적이 나아지도록 공부 방법을 바꿨어요.
皆がわかるようにグラフを見せて説明した。 모두가 이해하도록 그래프를 보여주면서 설명했어요.

Examples

A: 明日誕生日パーティーだよね？何時？

B: 8時だよ. 明日来てくれたら嬉しいな。

A: Tomorrow is your birthday party, isn't it? When?

明天是你的生日派对吧？几点？

B: 8'o clock. I hope you guys can come.

8点， 希望你们能来。

A: 내일 너의 생일 파티가 있지? 몇 시야?

B: 8시야. 내일 꼭 올 수 있기를 바라.

A: Teacher, I didn't do well on the exam.

C 老师, 我这次考得不太好。

K 선생님, 이번 시험을 잘 못 봤어요.

J 先生、今回の試験がよく見えませんでした。

B: That's okay. I hope you make progress on the next exam.

C 没关系！希望你下次考试有进步。

K 괜찮아요. 다음 시험에 더 잘 보기를 바라요.

J 大丈夫です。次の試験でよりよく見ることを願っています。

A: I'm going to study in Korea next week.

C 我下个星期要去韩国留学。

K 다음 주에 한국에 공부하러 가요.

J 来週韓国に勉強に行きます。

B: Amazing! I hope everything goes well in Korea.

C 太好了！祝你在韩国一切顺利。

K 잘 됐네요. 한국에서 모든 일이 잘 되기를 바라요.

J いいですね。韓国ですべてがうまくいくことを願っています。

A: I heard that you're going on a trip tomorrow. I wish you a safe journey.

C 听说明天你要去旅行，祝你一路平安。

K 내일 여행 간다고 들었어요. 안전한 여행 되기를 바라요.

J 明日旅行に行くと聞きました。安全な旅行になることを願っています。

B: Thank you.

C 谢谢。

K 고마워요.

J ありがとうございます。

Exercises

Here are some common wishes in life that people express to each other. Fill in the blanks based on each situation.

Happy Birthday!

C 生日快乐。

K 생일 축하해요.

J お誕生日おめでとうございます。

Happy New Year!

C 新年快乐。

K 새해 복 많이 받으세요.

J 明けましておめでとうございます。

Have a safe trip!

C 一路平安。

K 안전한 여행 되세요.

J 安全な旅に旅を or 旅になりますように。

All the best! (Everything goes smoothly with you.)

C 一切顺利。

K 소원성취하시길.

J よろしくお願いします。

Get well soon!

C 早日康复。

K 곧 회복하시기를 바랍니다.

J お早い回復を願っております。

I hope you find your dream job!

C 找到满意的工作。

K 원하는 직장 찾기를 바랍니다.

J ご希望の職場を探してください。

1. A: Today is your birthday. I wish you ____________!

C 今天是你的生日，祝你 ____________。

K 오늘 생일이지요? 생일축하해요.

J 今日の誕生日ですか？お誕生日おめでとうございます。

B: Thank you!

C 谢谢。

K 고맙습니다.

J ありがとう。

2. A: New year is around the corner. I wish you ____________!

C 新年快到了！祝你 ____________, ____________!

K 곧 새해가 되네요. ____________

J まもなく新年になりますね。 ____________.

B: Thank you! I also wish you ____________!

C 谢谢，也祝你 ____________!

K 고마워요. ____________.

J ありがとうございます。 ____________.

3. A: I cannot make it to class. I'm sick today.

C 我今天生病了，没法来上课。

K 오늘 몸이 안 좋네요. 오늘 수업에 갈 수 없을 것 같아요.

J 今日病気です。今日は授業に行けないと思います。

B: That's okay. I hope you ____________!

C 没关系。希望你 ____________！

K 괜찮아요. ____________.

J 大丈夫。 ____________。

4. A: My son is going to graduate from college soon.

C 我儿子马上就要大学毕业了。

K 제 아들이 곧 대학을 졸업해요.

J 息子はもうすぐ大学を卒業します。

B: I hope he ____________!

C 希望他 ____________！

K ____________기를 바랍니다.

J 彼が ____________であることを願っています!

Exercise

You will do the following for….

1. ____________ように勉強しています。

2. ____________ように働きます。

3. ____________電話します。

4. ________________________運動します。

5. ________________________タクシーに乗ります。

V+于 to, from, at: indicating origin

V+于 is a structure that originates from classical Chinese and is now only used in formal or written language. V+于 generally indicates the origin of something. In spoken Chinese, "是从……来的" or "是在……V的" is used to introduce the origin. I.e. 归于他 means "belongs to him". "本于他" means "originates from him". In Korean, the corresponding forms vary. Refer to the translations below.

Some commonly used phrases are:

- 属于(shǔyú): belong to (used in both formal/casual context.), ~에 속하다.

  This piece of clothes doesn't belong to me. I can't take it.

  C 这件衣服不属于我, 我不能拿。

  K 이 옷은 저에게 속한 아니라서 가져갈 수 없어요.

  J この服は私のものじゃありません。持っていくことはできません。

● 毕业于(bìyèyú) : graduate from, ~에서 졸업하다.

In formal context:

I graduated from the department of East Asian Studies at NYU.

C 我毕业于纽约大学东亚系。

K 저는 뉴욕대학 동아시아학에서 졸업했어요.

J ニューヨーク大学の東アジア研究学科を卒業しました。

In casual context:

C 我是从纽约大学东亚系毕业的。

K 저는 뉴욕대학 동아시아학으로 졸업했어요.

J ニューヨーク大学の東アジア研究学科を出ました。

● 出生于(chūshēngyú) : to be born at(location/time), ~에서 태어나다 ~で生まれる

In formal context:

I was born in Tokyo in the 80's.

C 我出生于80年代的东京。

K 80년대에 동경에서 태어났어요.

J 八十年代に東京で誕生しました。

In casual context:

C 我是在80年的东京出生的。

K 80년대 동경에서 태어났어요.

J 八十年代に東京で生まれました。

● 来自于(láizìyú)：come from, originate from, ~에서 오다.

In formal context:

This sentence comes from a very popular TV show.

C 这句话来自于一个很红的电视。

K 이 문장은 아주 인기있는 텔레비전에서 가져 온 것이에요.

J この文章は大変人気があるテレビ番組からきています。

In casual context:

C 这句话是从一个很红的电视来的。

K 이 문장은 아주 인기있는 텔레비전에서 따 온 거예요.

J この文章は大変人気があるテレビ番組からきています。

Exercise

Choose the appropriate words to fill in the blanks.

属于、毕业于、出生于、来自于

1. The students at NYU come from all over the world. Therefore the culture is very diverse.

C 纽约大学的学生__________全世界各地，有很多元的文化。

K 뉴욕대학 학생들은 전세계에서 와서 문화가 아주 다양해요.

J ニューヨーク大学の学生は世界中から来ている。それで、文化は多様である。’

2. The interns in this company all graduated from the famous colleges in the U.S.. Everyone is superb.

C 这家公司的实习生都________美国名牌大学，个个都很厉害。

K 이 회사의 인턴들은 모두 미국의 유명한 대학에서 졸업해서 뛰어나요.

J この会社のインターンはアメリカの有名な大学を卒業した人ばかりだ。皆とても優秀だ。

3. Even though he was born in the rural area, he has some progressive ideas.

C 虽然他__________农村，但是思想很前卫。

K 비록 시골에서 태어났지만 아주 진보적이에요.

J 田舎出身だが、進歩的な考えをしている。

4. Korean class belongs to the Department of East Asian Studies, so you should go to its website to find out more about the Korean class.

C 韩文课____________东亚系，所以你应该在东亚系的网站上看看韩文课的资料。

K 한국어 수업은 동아시아학과에 속해서 웹사이트에 가면 한국어 수업에 대한 좀 더 많은 정보를 찾을 수 있어요.

J 韓国語のクラスは東アジア研究学科なので、ウェブサイトで情報を調べた方がいいですよ。

24

Romans/로마서/罗马书/ローマ人への手紙

12:1, 2

Therefore, I urge you, brothers and sisters, in view of God's mercy, to offer your bodies as a living sacrifice, holy and pleasing to God—this is your true and proper worship. Do not conform to the pattern of this world, but be transformed by the renewing of your mind. Then you will be able to test and approve what God's will is—his good, pleasing and perfect will.

형제자매 여러분, 그러므로 나는 하나님의 자비하심을 힘입어 여러분에게 권합니다. 여러분의 몸을 하나님께서 기뻐하실 거룩한 산 제물로 드리십시오. 이것이 여러분이 드릴 합당한 예배입니다. 여러분은 이 시대의 풍조를 본받지 말고, 마음을 새롭게 함으로 변화를 받아서, 하나님의 선하시고 기뻐하시고 완전하신 뜻이 무엇인지를 분별하도록 하십시오.

所以，弟兄们， 我以 神的慈悲劝你们，
Suǒyǐ，dìxiōngmen，wǒ yǐ shén de cíbēi quàn nǐmen,
将身体献上， 当作活祭， 是圣洁的，
jiāng shēntǐ xiànshàng，dàng zuò huó jì，shì shèngjié de,
是神所喜悦的； 你们如此事奉乃是理所当然的。
shì shén suǒ xǐyuè de；nǐmen rúcǐ shì fèng nǎi shì lǐsuǒdāngrán de.
不要效法这个世界， 只要心意更新而变化，
Bùyào xiàofǎ zhège shìjiè，zhǐyào xīnyì gēngxīn ér biànhuà,

叫你们察验何为 神的善良、　　　　纯全、
jiào nǐmen cháyàn hé wèi shén de shànliáng, chún quán,
可喜悦的旨意。
kě xǐyuè de zhǐyì.

兄弟(きょうだい)たちよ。そういうわけで、神(かみ)のあわれみによってあなたがたに勧(すす)める。あなたがたのからだを、神(かみ)に喜(よろこ)ばれる、生(い)きた、聖(せい)なる供(そな)え物(もの)としてささげなさい。それが、あなたがたのなすべき霊的(れいてき)な礼拝(れいはい)である。
あなたがたは、この世(よ)と妥協(だきょう)してはならない。むしろ、心(こころ)を新(あら)たにすることによって、造(つく)りかえられ、何(なに)が神(かみ)の御(ご)旨(むね)であるか、何(なに)が善(ぜん)であって、神(かみ)に喜(よろこ)ばれ、かつ全き(まった)きことであるかを、わきまえ知(し)るべきである。

Chinese

慈悲: mercy, あわれみ, 자비하심

劝: to urge, すす-める [勧める], 권하다

身体: body, からだ, 몸

献上: to offer, ささげる, 드리다

当作: as~, ~として, ~로 (~로 삼아)

活: to live, い-きる [生きる·活きる], 살다

祭: sacrifice, くもつ [供物], 제물

圣洁: to be holy, せいなる [聖なる], 거룩하다

喜悦: to please, よろこ-ぶ [喜ぶ], 기뻐하다

事奉 : to serve, らいはい [礼拝], 예배

效法: to conform, みなら-う [見習う], 본받다

世界 : world, よ [世], 세상

心意: mind, こころ [心], 마음

新: new, あらたに [新たに], 새롭게

变化: to change, かえる [変える], 변화시키다

察验: to inspect and test, わきまえ [弁え], 분별하다

旨意: will, むね [宗·旨], 뜻

善良: good, ぜん [善], 선

Japanese

そういう: such, 那 [nà], 그런

あわれみ: mercy, 慈悲 [cíbēi], 자비

勧める: to urge, 劝 [quàn], 권하다

からだ: body, 身体 [shēntǐ], 몸

喜ばれる: to be pleased, 喜悦 [xǐyuè], 기뻐하다

生きる: to live, 活 [huó], 살다

聖なる: to be holy, 圣洁 [shèngjié], 거룩하다

供え物: sacrifice, 祭 [jì], 제물

ささげる: to offer, 献上 [xiànshàng], 드리다

べき [可き]: should, 需要 [xūyào], 해야하다

礼拝: worship, 事奉 [shìfèng], 예배

妥協: to compromise, 妥协 [tuǒxié], 타협하다

むしろ [寧ろ]: rather, 干脆 [gāncuì], 차라리

心: mind, 心意 [xīnyì], 마음

新たに: newly, 新 [xīn], 새롭게

造る: to make, 造 [zào], 만들다

か-える [変える]: to change, 变 [biàn], 바꾸다

なにが [何が]: why, 为什么 [wèishén · me], 어째서

御旨: God's will, 旨意 [zhǐyì], 하나님의 뜻

善: good, 善良 [shànliáng], 선

よろこ-ぶ [喜ぶ]: to please, 喜悦 [xiyuè], 기뻐하다

か-つ [勝つ]: to win, 胜 [shèng], 이기다

全き: perfect, 完全 [wánquán], 완전

わきまえ [弁え]: to inspect and test, 察验 [cháyàn], 분별하다

知る: to know, 知 [zhī], 알다

Korean

자비하다: mercy, 慈悲 [cíbēi], あわれみ

힘입다: to owe, 得到帮助 [dédàobāngzhù], お-う [負う]

권하다: to urge, 劝 [quàn], すす-める [勧める]

몸: body, 身体 [shēntǐ], からだ

기뻐하다: to be pleased, 喜悦 [xǐyuè], よろこ-ぶ [喜ぶ]

거룩하다: to be holy, 圣洁 [shèngjié], せいなる [聖なる]

살다: to live, 活 [huó], い-きる [生きる·活きる]

제물: sacrifice, 祭 [jì], くもつ [供物]

드리다: to offer/give (honorific), 奉 [fèng], ささ-げる [捧げる]

합당하다: to be appropriate, 适当 [shìdàng], 当を得る [とうをえる]

예배: worship, 事奉 [shìfèng], らいはい [礼拝]

시대: generation, 时代 [shídài], じだい [時代]

풍조: trend, ふうちょう [風潮], 潮流 [cháoliú]

본받다: to conform, 效法 [xiàofǎ], みなら-う [見習う]

지 말다: should not (prohibition), 不可 [bùkě], ならない

마음: mind, 心意 [xīnyì], こころ [心]

새롭게: newly, 新 [xīn], あらたに [新たに]

변화: change, 变化 [biànhuà], へんか [変化]

받다: to receive, 受 [shòu], 受ける [うける]

선하다: to be good, 善良 [shànliáng], よ-い [良い·善い]

완전하다: to be perfect, 完全 [wánquán], まったき [全き]

기뻐하다: to be pleased, 喜悦 [xǐyuè], よろこ-ぶ [喜ぶ]

분별하다: to inspect, 察验 [cháyàn], わきまえ [弁え]

Korean deferential style

ㅂ/습니다, ㅂ/십니까?, ~(으)십시오, ㅂ/읍시다

This style expresses the highest degree of respect to the addressee. It is usually spoken in historical dramas and in business settings such as customer service, conference presentations, and broadcastings (TV news). It can be mixed with the polite style (~아/어요).

	statement	question	command	proposition
Consonant-ending stem	앉습니다 (I) sit.	앉으십니까 ? (Do you) sit?	앉으십시오 Please sit.	앉읍시다 Let's sit down.
Vowel-ending stem	가십니다 (I) go.	가십니까 ? (Do you) go?	가십시오 Please go.	가십시다 Let's go.

In a restaurant, a waiter and a customer

종업원: 손님, 어서 오십시오. 무엇을 드시겠습니까?

Hello. Welcome. Are you ready to order?

いらっしゃいませ。ご注文は何になさいますか。

손님: 두부 전골 주십시오. 맵지 않게 해 주세요.

Tofu Jeongol, please. And please make it not spicy.

お豆腐のチョンゴルをお願いします。辛くしないでください。

In broadcasting, a reporter and an interviewee

기자: 이번 설 명절에 고향에 내려갈 생각이십니까?

Are you going to visit your hometown for this New Year's holiday?

お正月のお休みは田舎にお帰りになりますか。

인터뷰 대상자: 아니요, 코로나 때문에 고향에 갈 수 없을 것 같습니다.

No, I wouldn't be able to do so due to COVID.

コロナだから行けないでしょうね。

Exercise

1. Let's start the conference now.

지금부터 회의를 (시작하다) ______________.

では、会議を________________。

2. Let me tell you today's news.

오늘 뉴스를 (말씀드리다) ______________.

では、今日のニュースを＿＿＿＿＿＿＿＿＿＿。

3. Please fasten your seat belt inside the airplane.
기내에서는 안전 벨트를 꼭 (매다) ＿＿＿＿＿＿＿＿.
シートベルトを＿＿＿＿＿＿＿＿＿＿。

4. What's the weather like tomorrow?
내일 날씨가 (어떻다) ＿＿＿＿＿＿＿＿?
明日の天気は＿＿＿＿＿＿＿＿＿＿。

5. Last year it was cold and snowed a lot.
작년에는 눈이 많이 오고 (춥다) ＿＿＿＿＿＿＿＿.
昨年は＿＿＿＿＿＿＿＿＿＿。

Activity

Introduce yourself using the deferential style.

Japanese Deontic modality べき

To convey the meaning of "ought to do something" or "should do something", the following structure is used in Japanese. For

Korean, ~어/아야 하다 is used for positive sentences, and ~(으)면 안 되다 for negative sentences ("ought not to do something" or "should not do something"). In Chinese, "应该" (should) is used to express the same meaning.

verb plain/short form affirmative + べきだ・べきです

	affirmative	negative
present	べきだ・です	べきじゃない・じゃありません
past	べきだった・でした	べきじゃなかった・じゃありませんでした。

1. Students ought to study.

J 学生は勉強する(or す) べきです。

K 학생은 공부해야 해요.

C 学生应该学习。

2. You should take responsibility and do it till the end.

J 責任を持って最後までやるべきです。

K 책임을 지고 끝까지 해야 해요.

C 你应该负责人做到最后。

3. You should not speak ill of people.

J 人の悪口は言うべきじゃない。
K 사람의 약점을 말하면 안 돼요.
C 你应该不要在别人背后说坏话。

In the case of adjectives and nouns,

「くある」is used at the end of いadjectives and「である」for な adjectives and nouns.

1. The instructions should be easy to understand for everyone.
J 使い方の説明は誰にも分かりやすくあるべきだ。
K 사용 설명은 누구나 이해할 수 있어야 해요.
C 这个使用说明应该让每个人都很容易懂。

2. Since this kitchen is new, it should be convenient.
J 新しいキッチンなのだからもっと便利であるべきだ。
K 새 부엌이니까 편리해야 해요.
C 因为这个厨房是新的，应该很方便。

Exercise

Express the following sentences in each of the three languages.

1. You should go to school every day.

2. You should think about the future of the earth.

3. People should not waste resources.

4. You should not lie.

5. You should be nice to people.

6. You should be honest.

7. Parents should be a good example for their children.

(应该, 해야 하다)

25

Romans/로마서/罗马书/ローマ人への手紙
14:8

If we live, we live for the Lord; and if we die, we die for the Lord. So, whether we live or die, we belong to the Lord.

우리는 살아도 주님을 위하여 살고, 죽어도 주님을 위하여 죽습니다. 그러므로 우리는 살든지 죽든지 주님의 것입니다.

我们若活着， 是为主而活； 若死了，
Wǒmen ruò huózhe, shì wéi zhǔ ér huó; ruò sǐle,
是为主而死。 所以，我们或活或死总 是主的人。
shì wéi zhǔ ér sǐ. Suǒyǐ, wǒmen huò huó huò sǐ zǒng shì zhǔ de rén.

わたしたちは、生(い)きるのも主のために生(い)きる、死(し)ぬのも主のために死(し)ぬ。だから、生(い)きるにしても死(し)ぬにしても、わたしたちは主のものなのである。

Chinese

若: if, もし [若し], 만약/만일

活: to live, い-きる [生きる], 살다

死: to die, し-ぬ [死ぬ], 죽다

为: for, のために, 을 위하여

或: either, あるいは [或いは], 혹

总是: always, かならず [必ず], 반드시

Japanese

もの: thing/person, ~的, 것/사람

生きる: to live, 活 [huó], 살다

のために: for, 为 [wèi], 을 위하여

死ぬ: to die, 死 [sǐ], 죽다

だから: therefore, 所以 [suǒyǐ], 그러므로

Korean

살다: to live, 活 [huó], い-きる [生きる]

위하여: for, 为 [wèi], ために

죽다: to die, 死 [sǐ], し-ぬ [死ぬ]

그러므로: therefore, 所以 [suǒyǐ], だから

Regardless of 不管，~して，~든지 ~든지

This form is used when two or more given situations are acceptable. For Korean usage, the given situations can be either a simple list of choices or more than one contradictory choice for the purpose of emphasis. In Chinese, 不管A还是B or 不管A不A (不管：bùguǎn, regardless of) is used to connect two contradictory choices, while 或者 (huòzhě,or) is used to connect non-contradictory choices. Japanese uses てform＋も in this case.

1. Whether we live or die, we belong to the Lord.

K 살든지 죽든지 주님의 것입니다.

C 不管我们生还是死，我们都是上帝的人。

J 生きるにしても死ぬにしても、私たちは主のものなのである。

2. A: What do you want for lunch?

K 점심으로 뭐 드시고 싶어요?

C 你午饭想吃什么？

J 昼ごはんは何が食べたい。

B: I'm starving to death. I want to eat anything delicious or not.

K 배가 고파 죽겠어요. 맛있든지 없든지 아무거나 먹고 싶어요.

C 我饿死了，不管好不好吃我都吃。

J すごくお腹が空いているから、おいしくてもおいしくなくてもなんでもいいから食べたい。

3. A: I'm going to a concert tomorrow, and the weather forecast said it's raining.

K 내일 콘서트에 가는데 일기예보에서 비가 온다고 했어요.

C 我明天去音乐会，天气预报说下雨。

J 明日コンサートに行くんですが、天気予報は雨だと言っています。

B: The concert is said to be held whether it rains or snows.

K 비가 오든지 눈이 오든지 콘서트가 열린대요.

C 听说不管下不下雨，音乐会都开。

J 雨が降っても、雪が降ってもコンサートは行われるそうですよ。

4. A: What do you plan to do for summer break?

K 여름 방학인데 뭐 할 거예요?

C 你暑假打算做什么？

J 夏休みには何をする予定ですか。

B: I am thinking to go on a camping trip or doing an internship.

K 캠핑 여행을 가든지 인턴십을 하든지 하려고요.

C 我考虑去野营或者做实习。

J キャンプに行くかインターンシップをするか考えています。

(이 문장은 둘 중의 하나를 하겠다는 뜻이다.)

Exercise

1. A: What is your favorite food?

K 좋아하는 음식이 뭐예요?

C 你喜欢吃什么？

J 好きな食べ物は何ですか。

B: I eat everything, whether it is Chinese, Japanese, or Korean food.

K ____________________ 다 좋아해요.

C ____________________, 我都喜欢吃。

J 中国料理でも、日本料理でも、韓国料理でも何でもよく食べます。

2. A: What kind of apartment are you looking for?

K 어떤 아파트를 찾고 있어요?

C 你在找什么样的公寓？

J どんなアパートを探していますか。

B: As long as it's clean, anything is okay, big or small.

K 깨끗하기만 하면 ____________________ 다 괜찮아요.

C ____________________, 只要干净就可以。

J きれいなら、大きくても小さくてもいいです。

3. A: Where do we meet this weekend?

K 주말에 어디서 만날까?

C 我们周末在哪里见面？

J 今週の週末はどこで会いましょうか。

B: A park or a coffee shop are both okay.

K ____________________ 다 괜찮아.

C ____________________ 都可以。

J 公園でもカフェでもどこでもいいですよ。

Activity

Describe your favorite food, apartment, roommate, and/or place, using ~든지 ~든지, or 不管/或者，……

为someone/something+而verb

expressing the purpose of an action

为……而……is a structure that originates from classical Chinese, and is now mainly used in a formal context. It either emphasizes the beneficiary of the action or expresses the purpose. In spoken Chinese, 为 can be replaced by 为了 and 而 can be omitted.

For Korean, the closest grammar components could be the construction verb + 기 위해 and noun + 을 위해. It can be used after adjectives are made into verbs by adding 어/아지다 (to become) so that the construction becomes 어/아 지기 위해.

In Japanese, ために is used the most often. This is realized as noun + のために or verb plain form + ために. ために is also used to give a reason. If the purpose does not involve action verbs such as わかる、できる、or ある，instead ように is used.

1. Everyone should fight for their dreams.

C 每个人都应为梦想而奋斗。

K 모든 사람들은 꿈을 위해 싸워야 해요.

J 夢に向かって頑張るべきだ。

2. Many Chinese parents live for their children.

C 很多中国父母为孩子而活。

K 많은 중국 사람들이 자식들을 위해 살아요.

J 中国人の親の多くは子供のために生きている。

3. I study Chinese diligently so that I can go to China.

C 我为了能去中国而努力学中文。

K 저는 중국에 가기 위해 중국어를 열심히 배워요.

J 中国へ行くために中国語を勉強している。

4. I study medicine for my parents.

C 我为了家人而去学医。

K 저는 부모님을 위해 의대에 가요.

J 親のために医学を勉強している。

5. My parents are sending me to study abroad so that I can receive a better education.

C 我的父母为了让我有更好的教育而送我来美国留学。

K 제 부모님은 제가 더 좋은 교육을 받게 하기 위해 저를 미국 유학 보내셨어요.

J 両親はいい教育を受けるために私を留学させた。(いい教育が受けられるように)

Exercise

1. Why do you study Chinese, Korean or Japanese?

你为什么学中文/韩文/日文？

我为了____________________而学中文/韩文/日文。

I study Chinese, Korean or Japanese so that ….

どうして中国語/韓国語/日本語を勉強しているんですか。

왜 중국어/한국어/일본어를 공부하세요?

2. Why do you think people need to work?

你觉得人为什么要工作？

我觉得人们为了____________________而工作。

I think people work in order to ….

どうして人は働くと思いますか。

왜 사람은 일한다고 생각하세요?

3. What have you done in order to make your parents happy?

你为了让父母高兴做过什么？

我为了让父母高高兴而____________。

両親を幸せにするために何をしましたか。(両親が幸せになるように)

부모님을 행복하게 하기 위해 무엇을 했어요?

4. What do you study? For whom do you study ? Or why do you study it?

你现在学什么专业?你为了谁而学?或者说你为什么学？

我为了____________而学____________。

何を勉強していますか。何のために勉強していますか。どうして勉強していますか。

무엇을 공부하세요? 무엇을 위해 공부하세요? 왜 공부하세요?

Activity

Make conversations with the above questions expressing your own thoughts.

26

Romans/로마서/罗马书/ローマ人への手紙
14:17

The kingdom of God is not a matter of eating and drinking, but of righteousness, peace and joy in the Holy Spirit.

하나님의 나라는 먹는 일과 마시는 일이 아니라, 성령 안에서 누리는 의와 평화와 기쁨입니다.

因为 神的国不在乎吃喝, 只在乎公义、 和平,
Yīnwèi shén de guó bùzàihū chīhē, zhǐ zàihū gōng yì, hépíng,
并圣灵中的喜乐。
bìng shènglíng zhōng de xǐlè.

神(かみ)の国(くに)は飲食(いんしょく)ではなく、義(ぎ)と、平和(へいわ)と、聖霊(せいれい)における喜(よろこ)びとである。

Chinese

在乎: to care about, 気にする, 신경쓰다

喝: to drink, の-む [飲む], 마시다

只: only, ただ, 다만

公义: righteousness, ぎ [義], 의

和平: peace, へいわ [平和], 평화

喜乐: joy, よろこび [喜び], 기쁨

Japanese

飲食: food, 饮食 [yǐnshí], 음식

義: righteousness, 公义 [gōngyì], 공의

平和: peace, 和平 [hépíng], 평화

と: and, 和 [hé], 와/과

喜び: joy, 喜乐 [xǐlè], 기쁨

Korean

먹다: to eat, 吃 [chī], く-う [食う]

일: work, 事 [shì], しごと [仕事]

마시다: to drink, 喝 [hē], の-む [飲む]

의: righteousness, 公义 [gōngyì], ぎ [義]

평화: peace, 和平 [hépíng], へいわ [平和]

기쁨: joy, 喜乐 [xǐlè], よろこび [喜び]

Korean dynamic locative particles 에서 (で)

There are two kinds of locative particles, 에 and 에서. 에 is used to indicate static location and 에서 to indicate dynamic location. When an event or action happens in a specific place, 에서 is added as a suffix to this location.

Similarly in Japanese, a location is marked by で when an action takes place there. To merely indicate a static location, に is used.

In modern spoken Chinese, no locative particle is used to indicate location. However, preposition 在 is commonly placed before the location word to introduce both static location and dynamic location.

1. The kingdom of God is a matter of righteousness, peace and joy in the Holy Spirit.

K 하나님의 나라는 성령 안에서 의와 평화와 기쁨을 누리는 것이다.

J 神の国は聖霊の中で義と平和と喜びを味わうのです。

C 因为 神的国不在乎吃喝，只在乎公义、和平， 并圣灵中的喜乐。

(The sentence is of formal written style, which is why a locative particle 乎 is used after 在, which is a verb meaning "exist" in this context and not a preposition.)

2. I ate breakfast at the bagel shop around the corner today.

K 오늘 골목에 있는 베이글 가게에서 아침을 먹었어요.

J 今日は角のベーグル屋さんで朝ごはんを食べた。

C 我今天在街角的贝果店吃早饭。

3. People are working at home because of COVID.

K 사람들이 요즘 코로나 때문에 집에서 일을 해요.

J コロナのために皆家で働いている。

C 因为疫情, 人们都在家上班。

Exercise

Make a full sentence using the given words.

1. library/to study

K 도서관/공부하다

J 図書館で勉強する

C 图书馆/学习

2. room/to study

K 방/공부하다

J 部屋で勉強する

C 房间/学习

3. sofa/to watch TV

K 소파/텔레비전 보다

J ソファに座ってテレビを見る

C 沙发上/看电视

4. bed/to sleep

K 침대/자다

J ベッドで寝る

C 床上/睡觉

5. classroom/to take class

K 교실/수업 듣다

J 教室で講義を受ける

C 教室/上课

Activity

Have a conversation with classmates about what they did and where they were yesterday.

Contrastive

不是A，而是B, Aではなく Bである，A(이/가) 아니라 B이다: It is not A, but B

This structure simply states that something is not A, but B. In Japanese, if A is not a noun, you add の at the end of the phrase (plain form) to make a noun phrase. In Korean, if A is a present tense verb, ~는 게 아니라 and a past tense verb/a present tense adjective ~(으)ㄴ 게 아니라 should be added to the stems to make noun phrases. In Chinese, the conjunction 而 is commonly placed between the two clauses to express contrast.

1. This word is not Japanese, but Chinese.

J この言葉は日本語ではなく、中国語だ。

C 这个词不是日文，是中文。

K 이 단어는 일본어가 아니라 중국어예요.

2. The reason I am going to France is not for fun but for work.

J フランスへ行く理由は楽しみではなく仕事だ。

C 去法国不是为了玩，而是为了工作。

K 프랑스에 가는 이유는 놀려고 가는 게 아니라 일하려고 가는 거예요.

3. It's not that Yamada cannot do this job, but that s/he does not want to do it.

J 山田さんは仕事ができないのではなくしたくないのだ。

C 不是山田先生不能做这份工作，而是不想做。

K 야마다 씨가 할 수 없는 게 아니라 하고 싶지 않은 거예요.

4. Lee didn't come to the meeting not because she forgot, but rather because she was sick.

J リーさんが会議に来なかったのは忘れたのではなく、病気だったからだ。

C 李没来开会不是因为她忘了，而是因为她病了。

K 이 선생이 모임에 안 온 것은 잊어버린 게 아니라 아프기 때문이에요.

Exercise

1. library/school

K 도서관/학교

J 図書館/学校

C 图书馆/学校

2. room/living room

K 방/거실

J 部屋/リビングルーム

C 房间/客厅

3. sofa/floor/to watch TV

K 소파/바닥/텔레비전을 보다

J ソファに/床に/座ってテレビを見る

C 沙发上/地面上/看电视

4. bed/floor/to sleep

K 침대/바닥/자다

J ベッドで/床で/寝る

C 床上/地面上/睡觉

5. classroom/to take class

K 교실/인터넷/수업 듣다

J 教室で/インターネットで/講義を受ける

C 教室/在网上/上课

27

1 Corinthians/고린도전서/哥林多前书/コリント人への手紙第一
1:18

For the message of the cross is foolishness to those who are perishing, but to us who are being saved it is the power of God.

십자가의 말씀이 멸망할 자들에게는 어리석은 것이지만, 구원을 받는 사람인 우리에게는 하나님의 능력입니다.

因为十字架的道理, 在那灭亡的人为愚拙；
Yīnwèi shízìjià de dàolǐ, zài nà mièwáng de rénwéi yúzhuō;
在我们得救的人, 却为 神的 大能。
zài wǒmen déjiù de rén, què wèi shén de dà néng.

十字架の言は、滅び行く者には愚かであるが、救にあずかるわたしたちには、神の力である。

WORD

Chinese

因为: because, なぜなら, 왜냐하면

十字架: the cross, じゅうじか [十字架], 십자가

道理: reason, どうり [道理], 도리

灭亡: to perish, ほろびる [滅びる], 멸망하다

愚拙: to be foolish, つたない [拙い], 어리석다

得: to gain, 得る [える], 얻다

救: to save, すく-う [救う], 구원하다

却: on the contrary, かえって, 도리어

为: to become, なる [為る], 되다

大能: power, ちから [力], 능력

Japanese

十字架: the cross, 十字架 [shízìjià], 십자가

滅びる: to perish, 灭亡 [mièwáng], 멸망하다

おろか [愚か]: foolishness, 愚 [yú], 어리석음

あずか-る [与る]: to make relation, 参预 [cānyù], 관여하다

救: to save, 救 [jiù], 구원하다

Korean

십자가: the cross, 十字架 [shízìjià], じゅうじか [十字架]

말씀: teaching, 道理 [dào · li], どうり [道理]

멸망하다: to perish, 灭亡 [mièwáng], ほろびる [滅びる]

자: person, 人 [rén], もの [者]

어리석다: to be foolish, 愚 [yú], ばからしい [馬鹿らしい]

구원: salvation, 救 [jiù], きゅうえん [救援]

능력: power, 能 [néng], ちから [力]

Contrastive connective ~지만 却/而 が

~지만 is the clausal connective form of the conjunction 그렇지만 or 하지만. It connects two clauses with contrasting meanings and expresses the speaker's surprise or an unexpected situation, emphasizing the second clause.

が is used in Japanese at the end of the first clause to express this meaning. Similarly, けど or けれども can used.

In Chinese, 却 is used to express the speaker's surprise or an unexpected situation, and 而 indicates a contrast between the first and second clause. Note that 却 is an adverb, and therefore should be placed after subject and before the verb. 而, on the other hand, is a conjunction, so it connects two clauses.

Examples

1. The message of the cross looks foolish, but it is the power of God. (unexpectedness)

K 십자가 말씀이 어리석어 보이지만 하나님의 능력입니다.

C 十字架的道理看似愚拙，却为 神的大能。

J 十字架の言は、滅び行く者には愚かであるが、神の力である

2. It is warm in Tokyo in March, but it is still cold in New York. (contrast)

K 3월에 토쿄는 따뜻하지만 뉴욕은 아직 추워요.

C 东京三月很暖和，而纽约还很冷。

J 東京は三月は暖かいが、ニューヨークはまだ寒い。

3. My roommate does not exercise, but is healthy. (unexpectedness)

K 룸메이트는 운동을 안 하지만 건강해요.

C 我的室友不锻炼却很健康。

J ルームメートは運動しないが、健康だ。

4. My family lives on Jeju Island, but I live in Seoul. (contrast)

K 제 가족은 제주도에 살지만 저는 서울에 살아요.

C 我的家人住在济州岛，而我住在首尔。

J 家族は済州島に住んでいますが、私はソウルに住んでいます。

Exercise

Connect or complete the sentences.

1. Jessica has short hair, but Amanda has long hair.

K 제시카는 머리가 짧아요. 하지만 아만다는 머리가 길어요.

C 杰西卡是短发。阿曼达是长发。

J ジェシカは髪が短いです。アマンダは髪が長いです。

2. My brother is young, but considerate.

K 제 동생은 나이가 어려요. 그렇지만 사려가 깊어요.

C 我弟弟很小。我弟弟很懂事。

J 弟はまだ若いです。思慮深いです。

3. It is cold in August in San Francisco, but it is warmer in January.

K 샌프란시스코는 8월에 추워요. 그렇지만 1월에 좀 더 따뜻해요.

C 旧金山八月很冷，而一月比较暖和。

J サンフランシスコは八月は寒いです。一月は暖かいです。

4. Korean food is spicy and salty, but ____________________.

K 한국 음식은 맵고 짜요.

→ ______________________________.

C 韩国料理又辣又咸____________________。

J 韓国料理は塩辛いです____________________。

5. I like action movies, but ______________________________.

K 저는 액션 영화를 좋아해요.

→ ______________________________________.

C 我喜欢动作片________________________________。

J アクション映画が好きです______________________。

6. Durian tastes good, but ___________________________.

K 두리안은 맛있어요.

→ ______________________________________.

C 榴莲很好吃__________________________________。

J ドリアンはおいしいです________________________。

Activity

Describe people/places around you using 지만.

(1) roommate / 룸메이트 / ルームメート / 室友

(2) best friend / 가장 친한 친구 / 親友 / 好友

(3) parents / 부모님 / 両親 / 父母

(4) hometown / 고향 / 出身 / 老家

(5) A favorite restaurant / 자주 가는 식당 / 一番好きなレストラン / 最喜欢的餐厅

How to make questions (1): Yes/No questions

Questions are used to ask for information, and there are several types of questions depending on the purpose of the inquiry. These include yes/no questions, rhetorical questions, and content questions. They will be introduced one by one.
All three languages, unlike English, have the same word order in both statements and questions.
In Korean, questions employ a rising tone in the final syllable, while the statements use a falling tone. When replying to yes/no questions, 네 for yes is followed by the repetition of the verbs and 아니요 for no is followed by the repetition of the verbs in the negative forms.

There are two ways to form a yes/no question in Chinese. One way is to add the question particle 吗 to the end of a statement. The other is to first use a verb in the positive then repeat the same verb in its negative form, similar to how in English we can say, "do you like soda or not", or "have you been there or not". This structure is realized as Verb-不/没-Verb, or Adjective-不/没-Adjective. However, when there are other components in the sentence such as an adverbial phrase describing time, location or manner of the action, only 吗-ending question can be used. When responding to either form of such yes/no questions, unlike in Japanese or Korean in which questions can simply be answered with "yes" or "no", it is much more natural to answer with a verb or adjective in its positive or negative form in Chinese. i.e. 喜欢(yes, I like it.), 不想(no, I don't want to do it.), 没吃(no, I haven't eaten.)

In Japanese, simply add a question marker か at the end of the sentence with a rising intonation. In the answer, start with "yes" (はい、ええ、うん etc.) and follow with the predicate part of the sentence, or "no" (いいえ、いえ、ううん etc.) and follow with the predicate in the negative form.

Examples

1. A: Are there many students in the class?

K 수업에 학생들이 많아요?

C 班上有很多学生吗？ or 班上有没有很多学生？

J 学生はクラスにたくさんいますか。

B: Yes, there are.

K 네, 많아요.

C 有，很多。

J はい、います。

2. A: Do you exercise every day?

- **K** 매일 운동해요?
- **C** 你每天都锻炼身体吗？
- **J** 毎日運動しますか。

B: No, I don't.

- **K** 아니요, 매일 운동 안 해요.
- **C** 不每天锻炼。
- **J** いいえ、しません。

3. A: Are you a graduate student?

- **K** 대학원생이에요?
- **C** 你是研究生吗？or 你是不是研究生？
- **J** 大学院生ですか。

B: No, I am not.

- **K** 아니요, 대학원생이 아니에요.
- **C** 不是(研究生)。
- **J** いいえ、大学院生じゃないです。

Exercise

Make questions and answers using given words in each of the three languages.

to cry, to be sick, to be a teacher, to run, to be happy, to be a doctor, to do work

哭，生病，做老师，跑步，高兴，做医生，工作

泣く、病気だ、先生だ、走る、幸せだ、医者だ、働く

Activity

Make yes/no questions and provide answers about your daily activities.

28

1 Corinthians/고린도전서/哥林多前书/コリント人への手紙第一
6:19, 20

Do you not know that your bodies are temples of the Holy Spirit, who is in you, whom you have received from God? You are not your own; you were bought at a price. Therefore honor God with your bodies.

여러분의 몸은 여러분 안에 계신 성령의 성전이라는 것을 알지 못합니까? 여러분은 성령을 하나님으로부터 받아서 모시고 있습니다. 여러분은 여러분 자신의 것이 아닙니다.

岂不知你们的身子就是圣灵的殿吗？
Qǐ bùzhī nǐmen de shēnzi jiùshì shènglíng de diàn ma?
这圣灵是从 神而来,　住在你们里头
Zhè shènglíng shì cóng shén ér lái,　zhù zài nǐmen lǐtou
的；并且你们不是自己的人，因为你们是重价买来的。
de;　bìngqiě nǐmen bùshì zìjǐ de rén,　yīnwèi nǐmen shì zhòng jià mǎi lái de.
所以，要在你们的　身子上荣耀 神。
Suǒyǐ,　yào zài nǐmen de　shēnzi shàng róngyào shén.

あなたがたは知(し)らないのか。自分(じぶん)のからだは、神(かみ)から受け(うけ)て自分(じぶん)の内(うち)に宿(やど)っている聖霊(せいれい)の宮(みや)であって、あなたがたは、もはや自分(じぶん)自身(じしん)のものではないのである。

Chinese

岂: how can it be (rhetorical question), どうやって, 어찌하여

不知: to not know, 知らない, 모르다

身子: body, からだ, 몸

里头: in, うち [内], 안

殿: temple, みや [宮], 성전

从: from, ~から, ~에서

住: to live, reside, おられる, 살다

并且: and, そして (また), 그리고 (또한)

因为: because, なぜなら, 왜냐하면

重价: high price, こうか[高価], 고가

买: to buy, か-う [買う], 사다

荣耀: glory, えいこう[栄光], 영광

Japanese

知る: to know, 知 [zhī], 알다

自分: self, 自己 [zìjǐ], 자기

からだ: body, 身子 [shēn · zi], 몸

受ける: to receive, 受 [shòu], 받다

内: in, 里头 [lǐ · tou], 안

宿る: to stay, 住 [zhù], 머물다

宮: temple, 殿 [diàn], 성전

もはや: already, 已经 [yǐ · jing], 이미

自身: self, 自身 [zìshēn], 자신

Korean

몸: body, 身子 [shēn · zi], からだ

성전: temple, 殿 [diàn], みや [宮]

것: thing, …的, もの

알다: to know, 知道 [zhī · dào], 知る [しる]

으로부터: from, 从 [cóng], ~から

받다: to receive, 受 [shòu], う-ける [受ける]

모시다: to serve, 侍奉 [shìfèng], つか-える [仕える·事える]

자신: self, 自身 [zìshēn], じしん [自身]

Referring to oneself 自己,自分(自身), 자기/자신/자기자신: reflexive pronouns

Reflexive pronouns are pronouns such as myself, yourself, herself, himself, itself, themselves, and ourselves. They are often used when the subject and the object of a verb are the same.

Korean has 자기, 자신, and 자기자신, which are semantically same and used in the following order of frequency: 자신>자기>자기자신.

Usually, the relevant personal pronouns occur prior to the reflexive pronoun. In Chinese, "自己"(zìjǐ) is used to refer to oneself. In Japanese, 自分、自身、自己 are used.

■ Examples

1. You are not your own.

K 여러분은 여러분 자신의 것이 아닙니다.

C 你不是你自己。

J 自分だけではない。

2. People need to know how to love themselves.

K 사람은 자기를 사랑할 줄 알아야 해요.

C 人们应该知道怎么爱自己。

J 自分自身を愛することを知らなくてはいけない。

3. Teacher: Hi everyone! Nice to meet you. Today. we'll have time to introduce ourselves.

K 학생 여러분 처음 뵙겠어요. 오늘은 자신을 소개하는 시간을 갖겠습니다.

C 老师：大家好！很高兴见到你们！今天我们会有时间介绍自己。

J 先生：皆さん、はじめまして。今日は自己紹介をしましょう。

Exercise

Translate from English to each of the three languages using reflexive pronouns.

1. I myself couldn't believe it.
2. Find a job that works for you.
3. My friend takes pride in his work.
4. College students learn to express their thoughts in writing.
5. I accidentally cut my finger while cooking last night.

How to make questions (2): rhetorical questions

A rhetorical question refers to a question that creates a dramatic effect with no answer expected. The answer is usually well known to both the speaker and the listener. It can also be used to form a question to the opposite of the speaker's intention, in which a different intonation is used from that of the regular question.
In Korean, a negative question with question words such as 누가, 언제, 어디서, 어떻게, 왜, 무엇을 is typically used as a rhetorical. The rhetorical question is also delivered with a falling intonation, emphasizing the speaker's intention.

Chinese rhetorical questions are mostly the same as Korean rhetorical questions, except that in Chinese rhetorical questions will end with a rising tone – the same as a typical Chinese question.

In Japanese, か, のか, or でしょうか is used with a falling intonation. To confirm, ね is used.

1. Do you not know you are the temple of the Holy Spirit? (You know so.)

K 여러분이 성령의 전이라는 것을 알지 않아요?

C 岂不知你们的身子就是圣灵的殿吗？

J 精霊の宮であることを知っているのか。

2. How nice the weather is! (It is so nice.)

K 오늘 날씨 좋지 않아요?

C 天气不好吗？

J すごくいい天気ですね。

3. Who wouldn't want to travel to New York? (Everyone wants to travel to New York)

K 누가 뉴욕에 여행가고 싶지 않을까요?

C 谁不想去纽约旅游？

J 誰がニューヨークに旅行したいでしょうか。

4. When will such an opportunity come? (It never comes again.)

K 언제 그런 기회가 올까요?

C 什么时候会再有这样的机会呢？

J いつそんな機会がやってくるのか。

Exercise

Fill in the blanks with a translation for the rhetorical question in each of the three languages.

1. A: You speak Chinese very well.

K 중국어를 참 잘 하시네요.

C 你中文说得很好。

J 中国語が上手ですね。

B: Am I good at Chinese? There are a lot of people who are good at it.

K ________________. 중국어를 잘 하는 사람이 많아요.

C ________________。 中文好的人很多。

J ________________。 中国語が上手でしょうか。そういう人はたくさんいる。

2. A: Would you like to come to my birthday party next week?

K 다음 주 제 생일 파티에 오실래요?

C 下个星期我的生日派对你来吗？

J 来週、私の誕生日パーティーに来たいですか。

B: Can't I go?

K 나는 가면 안 되나요?

C ______________________________?

J 行ってもいいですか。

3. A: I left my wallet at the restaurant yesterday. I have my ID and cash in my wallet.

K 어제 지갑을 식당에 두고 나왔어. 신분증하고 현금도 들어 있는데.

C 昨天我把钱包落在餐馆了, 钱包里有我的身份证和现金。

J 昨日レストランに財布を忘れてきてしまったんです。 身分証明書と現金が入っているんですが。

B: It would be nice if the person who picked it up returned it.

K 주운 사람이 돌려주면 좋을텐데.

C 要是捡到的人把钱包归还给你就好了。

J 拾った人が届けてくれたらいいんですが。

A: Where could such a person be?

K 그런 사람이 있을까?

C ______________________________?

J そんな人がいるでしょうか。

B: Don't think negatively, just wait.

K 부정적으로 생각하지 말고 기다려 봐.

C 别这么想, 等等看吧。

J そんなに否定的に考えないで、待ったらどうですか。

4. A: Shall we watch this movie together?

K 이 영화 같이 볼래요?

C 我们要一起看这部电影吗？

J 映画を一緒にみませんか。

B: Who wouldn't like to see it?

K 누가 그 영화를 보고 싶지 않겠어요?

C ______________________________？

J そんな映画、誰がみたいのでしょうか。

29

1 Corinthians/고린도전서/哥林多前书/コリント人への手紙第一
12:3

Therefore I want you to know that no one who is speaking by the Spirit of God says, "Jesus be cursed," and no one can say, "Jesus is Lord," except by the Holy Spirit.

그러므로 나는 여러분에게 알려드립니다. 하나님의 영으로 말하는 사람은 아무도 "예수는 저주를 받아라"라고 말할 수 없고, 또 성령을 힘입지 않고서는 아무도 "예수는 주님이시다"라고 말할 수 없습니다.

所以我告诉你们，　被　神的灵感动的，
Suǒyǐ wǒ gàosù nǐmen, bèi shén de línggǎndòng de,
没有说　「耶稣是可咒诅」的；若不
méiyǒu shuō `yēsū shì kě zhòu zǔ'de; ruò bù
是被圣灵感动的，　也没有能说　「耶稣是主」的。
shì bèi shènglíng gǎn dòng de, yě méiyǒu néng shuō `yēsū shì zhǔ'de.

そこで、あなたがたに言(い)っておくが、神(かみ)の霊(れい)によって語(かた)る者(もの)はだれも「イエスはのろわれよ」とは言(い)わないし、また、聖霊(せいれい)によらなければ、だれも「イエスは主(しゅ)である」と言(い)うことができない。

Chinese

所以: therefore, だから, 그러므로

告诉: to inform, しら-せる [知らせる], 알려주다

被: to be done (passive marker), …れる, …어/아 지다

感动: to be touched, かん-ずる [感ずる], 감동하다

说: to speak, かたる [語る], 말하다

咒诅: to curse, のろう [呪う], 저주하다

若: if, もし [若し], 만약

也: also, また, 또

Japanese

そこで: so, 所以 [suǒyǐ], 그래서

言う: to speak, 说 [shuō], 말하다

お-く: to put, 置 [zhì], 두다

よって: depending on, 依 [yī], ~에 의하여/인하여

語る: to speak, 说 [shuō], 말하다

のろ-う: to curse, 咒诅 [zhòuzǔ], 저주하다

また: and, 并且 [bìngqiě], 또

こと: thing, …的, 것

で-きる: can, 可以 [kěyǐ], 할 수 있다

Korean

그러므로: therefore, 所以 [suǒyǐ], だから

알려주다: to inform, 告诉 [gào · su], しら-せる [知らせる]

말하다: to speak, 说 [shuō], かたる [語る]

저주: curse, 咒诅 [zhòuzǔ], じゅそ [呪詛]

받다: to receive, 受 [shòu], う-ける [受ける]

힘입다: to owe, 得到帮助 [dédàobāngzhù], お-う [負う]

Ability/permission 能/会/可以, できる/できない, ~을 수 있다/없다

The modal verb 能 is placed before a verb in Chinese to express ability or permission. However, for acquired certain skills, 会 is used instead. 可以 is another word that can mean "can". It's generally used to express a suggestion of a particular activity when conditions permit.

In Japanese and Korean, できる, ~을 수 있다 occur after a verb to express possibility and/or ability in common. The Japanese structure is verb plain affirmative + ことができる

You can say "Jesus is Lord" by the Holy Spirit.

K 성령을 힘 입어서 "예수는 주님이시다"하고 말할 수 있어요.

C 被圣灵感动的能说「耶稣是主」。

J 「イエスは主(しゅ)である」と言うことができる。

1. A: Can you play the piano?

K 피아노 칠 수 있어요?

C 你会弹钢琴吗？(弹钢琴 is an acquired skill.)

J ピアノを弾くことができますか。

B: No, I can't, but I want to learn.

K 아니요, 칠 수 없지만 배우고 싶어요.

C 不会，但是我想学。

J できません。でも、習いたいです。

A: Everyone is capable of learning the piano if they want to.

K 원하기만 하면 아무나 배울 수 있어요.

C 每个人都能学, 要是他们想的话。

J 誰でも習いたかったら習うことができます。

2. A: Can you speak Japanese?

K 일본어를 말할 수 있어요?

C 你会说日文吗？

J 日本語を話すことができますか。

B: Yes, I can speak very well. However, I can't speak Japanese to my parents as they don't know the language.

K 네, 말할 수 있어요. 그런데 부모님께서 일본어를 말하실 수 없기 때문에 부모님하고는 말할 수 없어요.

C 会，我能说得很好。可是我不能跟父母说日文，因为他们不会。

J はい、上手に話すことができます。でも、日本語が分からないので、両親に話すことはできません。

3. A: What are we doing this weekend?

K 이번 주말에 뭐 할까?

C 我们这个周末做什么？

J 今週の週末は何をしましょうか。

B: If the weather is nice, we could take a walk in the park.

K 날씨가 좋으면 공원에서 산책할 수 있어.

C 天气好的话，我们可以去公园走走。

J 天気がよかったら公園で散歩することができます。

Exercise

Make sentences using the given keywords and the grammar structures for ability/permission

1. CAN DO (use 可以 for Chinese expressions)

park/nice weather/to cook BBQ

K 공원/날씨가 좋다/바베큐 하다

C 公园/好天气/烧烤

J 公園/いい天気/バーベキューする

2. Last weekend/to have free time/to hike

K 지난 주말/ 시간이 있다/하이킹하다

C 上个周末/有空/爬山

J 先週の週末/ひま/ハイキングする

3. CANNOT DO (중국어 能을 사용하세요.)

To snow a lot/to go to school

K 눈이 많이 오다/ 학교에 가다

C 下大雪/上学

J 大雪/学校に行く

4. To not have battery/to make a call to you

K 배터리가 없다/전화하다

C 手机没电了/打电话给你

J 電池がない/電話する

Activity

List three or more things and make conversation about what you can/can't do in the given situations.

(1) In the Grand Canyon National Park

(2) In the public library

(3) When you become 21 years old or more in US/China/Japan/

Korea

(4) When you become a parent

Japanese sustention aspect て おく , 어/아 두다/놓다, 提前

This form is used to mean "to get something done in anticipation of later use". おく means 'to put, to place, to keep' when used as a main verb, and became abstracted as an auxiliary verb in this construction.

て form of a verb + おく

本を読んでおく (read a book ahead of time)
名前を覚えておく (remember the name ahead of time)
窓を開けておく (leave the window open)
電気をつけておく leave the light on)

The Korean 두다 is exactly the same as the Japanese おく. 어/아 두다 can be replaced with 어/아 놓다 and 놓다, meaning 'to put down' as a main verb. Like in Japanese, these verbs are abstracted to denote the sustention aspect.

However, there is no similar use in Chinese. When a person needs to describe doing things ahead of time, adverb 先 or 事先 can be inserted before a verb in a sentence. When describing the action of preparing something ready for a later event, verb complement 好 commonly used.

Examples

1. I'll tell you.

K 여러분에게 말해 둡니다.

C 我告诉你们。

J あなたがたに言っておく.

2. A: I will go to Osaka next year.

K 내년에 오사카에 갈 거예요.

C 我们明年去大阪。

J 来年大阪にいきます。

B: That's nice. Flight tickets are cheap if you buy them in advance.

K 잘 됐네요. 비행기 표를 미리 사두면 싸요.

C 真好！要是你提前买，机票很便宜。

J いいですね。飛行機の切符は早めに買っておくと安いですよ。

3. I will clean the room in advance since my friend is coming to visit.

K 친구가 와서 방을 미리 청소해 놓으려고 해요.

C 因为我朋友要来，我得提前打扫好房间。

J 友達が来るから、部屋を掃除しておきます。

4. I will buy food and drink ahead of time for the party.

K 파티를 위해 음식하고 음료수를 사놓으려고 해요.

C 我会提前买一些派对上要吃的要喝的。

J パーティーのために飲み物や食べ物を買っておきます。

5. It would be a problem if we forget. Let's write it down.

K 잊어버리면 곤란하니까 써놓아요.

C 我们先写下来吧，要是忘了就麻烦了。

J 忘れると困るから、書いておきましょう。

30

2 Corinthians/고린도후서/哥林多后书/コリント人への手紙第二ー
4:5

For what we preach is not ourselves, but Jesus Christ as Lord, and ourselves as your servants for Jesus' sake.

우리는 우리 자신을 전하는 것이 아니라, 예수 그리스도를 주님으로 선포합니다. 우리는 예수로 말미암아 우리 자신을 여러분의 종으로 내세웁니다.

我们原不是传自己，乃是传基督耶稣为主，
Wǒmen yuán bùshì chuán zìjǐ, nǎi shì chuán jīdū yēsū wéi zhǔ,
并且自己因耶稣作你们的仆人。
bìngqiě zìjǐ yīn yēsū zuò nǐmen de púrén.

しかし、わたしたちは自分(じぶん)自身(じしん)を宣(の)べ伝(つた)える)のではなく、主(しゅ)(おも)なるキリスト・イエスを宣(の)べ伝(つた)える。わたしたち自身(じしん)は、ただイエスのために働(はたら)くあなたがたの僕(ぼく)にすぎない。

Chinese

原: originally, もともと [元元], 원래

传: to deliver, つたえる [伝える], 전하다

乃是: rather, かえって, 오히려

为: to become, なる [為る], 되다

主: Lord, しゅ [主], 주

因: for someone's sake, ~ために, ~로 말미암아

作: to make, つくる [作る], 만들다

仆人: servant, ぼく [僕], 종

Japanese

宣する: to preach, 宣布 [xuānbù], 선포하다

伝える: to transfer, 传 [chuán], 전하다

主: Lord, 主 [zhǔ], 주

なる: to be, 为 [wèi], 되다

ただ: only, 只 [zhī], 다만

働く: to work, 工作 [gōngzuò], 일하다

僕: servant, 仆人 [púrén], 종

Korean

전하다: to transfer, 传 [chuán], つた-える [伝える]

선포하다: to preach, 宣布 [xuānbù], せん-する [宣する]

말미암다: to be derived from, 经过 [jīngguò], へる [経る]

종: servant, 仆人 [púrén], ぼく [僕]

내세우다: to nominate, 使…站出 [shǐ...zhànchulai], かか-げる [掲げる]

Contrast conjunctions しかし, 不过/可是/但是, 하지만

Conjunctions vary extensively depending on sentential relations such as addition, contrast, cause-effect, exemplification, sequence, conclusion, elaboration, etc.

Conjunctions used to indicate contrast in Japanese are しかし、でも、けれど、and けれども. しかし is most commonly used in written language or formal situations, followed by けれども, けれど, and でも. These conjunctions come at the beginning of the second sentence. けど and が are used in the middle when the contrast is phrased in one sentence.

In Chinese, 不过, 可是 or 但是 are the most common conjunctions to indicate contrast. These words are generally used interchangeably. The Korean 하지만 can be shortened to the suffix ~지만 with verb/

adjective conjugation. Other contrast conjunctions include 그러나, 그렇지만, and 그런데.

Examples

1. He was once a famous singer, but now few people remember him.

K 그는 한때 유명한 가수였어요. 하지만 (→ 가수였지만) 지금은 기억하는 사람이 거의 없어요.

C 他以前是一名有名的歌手, 可是现在很少人记得。

J あの人はかつては有名な歌手だったが、今は覚えている人も少ない。

2. There is no entrance fee to this museum, but you can't touch anything.

K 이 박물관은 입장료가 없어요. 그렇지만 (→ 없지만) 아무것도 만지면 안돼요.

C 这家博物馆没有门票费，不过你什么东西都不能碰。

J この博物館は入場料はありません。でも、何も触ってはいけません。

3. A: It's raining hard, but I don't have an umbrella.

K 비가 많이 오네요. 하지만 (→ 오지만) 저는 우산이 없어요.

C 雨下得很大，但是我没伞。

J どしゃ降りですね。でも、傘がないんです。

B: Please use mine. I can leave later when it stops.

K 제 것 쓰세요. 비가 그치면 나중에 가도 돼요.

C 用我的吧。我可以等晚点雨停了再走。

J 私のを使ってください。私は雨が止んだら出ますから。

Exercise

Make connections between A and B using contrast conjunctions.

A: I am a cook. 요리사예요. 我是厨师。 コックです。

I love my dog. 개를 좋아해요. 我很爱我的狗。犬が好きです。

The hotel is nice. 호텔이 좋아요. 这个宾馆很不错。ホテルはいいです。

Spring break begins. 봄방학이 시작돼요. 春假开始了。春休みが始まります。

The weather is good. 날씨가 좋아요. 天气很好。天気がいいです。

B: It's expensive. 비싸요. 很贵。高いです。

I have a pollen allergy. 꽃가루 알레르기가 있어요. 我对花粉过敏。花粉症です。

I don't cook at home. 집에서 요리 안 해요. 我不能在家做饭。家で料理します。

I have to work for my part-time job. 아르바이트 해야 돼요. 我得打工。アルバイトをしなくてはいけません。

I hate it when he eats toilet paper. 화장지를 먹으면 싫어요. 他吃卫生纸的时候很讨厌。トイレットペーパーを食べるのがいやです。

Activity

Make conversations about contrasting cultural differences.

How to make questions 3: content questions

A content question is a question by which the speaker asks the listener to supply specific information about a person, object, time, location, reason, quantity, etc. It usually uses so-called 5W1H question words. Note that while WH-question pronouns always appear in the beginning of sentences in English, their word order can vary in Chinese, Japanese and Korean.

	Who	What/What kind of	When	Where	Why	How much/ many
Chinese	谁 shéi	什么 shénme / 哪种 nǎzhǒng	什么时候 shénmeshíhou / 几点 jǐdiǎn	哪里 nǎlǐ	为什么 wèishénme	几 jǐ / 多少 duōshǎo / 多 +adj.
Korean	누가	뭐 / 어떤	언제 / 몇시에	어디	왜	몇 / 얼마
Japanese	誰（だれ）	何 / どんな	いつ	どこ	なぜ、どうして	いくら いくつ

1. Person

Who bought this? (subject)

K 누가 이것을 샀어요?

C 这是谁买的？

J 誰がこれを書きましたか。

Who do you like among the BTS members? (object)

K BTS 중에서 누구를 좋아해요?

C BTS的成员中, 你喜欢谁？

J BTSの中で誰が好きですか。

2. Object

What is this?

K 이게 뭐예요?

C 这是什么？

J これは何ですか。

What kind of movies do you like?

K 어떤 영화를 좋아해요?

C 你喜欢哪种电影？

J どんな映画が好きですか。

3. Time

When is your vacation?

K 휴가가 언제예요? Or 언제 휴가예요?

C 你什么时候放假？

J 休みはいつですか。

What time do we meet?

K 몇 시에 만나요?

C 我们几点见？

J いつ会いますか。

4. Location

Where is your workplace?

K 직장이 어디에요?

C 你在哪里工作？

J どこで働いていますか。

Where are you from?

K 어느 지방에서 오셨어요?

C 你从哪里来的？

J 出身はどこですか。

5. Reason

Why do you learn Chinese?

K 왜 중국어를 배우세요?

C 你为什么学中文？

J どうして中国語を勉強しましか。

What made you come here?

K 어떤 일로 오셨어요?

C 你为什么来这里？

J どうしてここに来たんですか。

6. Quantity

How much is this?

K 이거 얼마예요?

C 这个多少钱？

J いくらですか。

How many students are in your class?

K 수업에 학생이 몇 명이 있어요?

C 你班上有几个学生？

J クラスに何人いますか。

How big is the park?

K 공원이 얼마나 커요?

C 这个公园多大？

J 公園はどのくらい大きいですか。

Exercise

Fill in the blank with an appropriate question word.

1. A: How do you learn Japanese?

평소에 ______________ 일본어를 배우세요?

B: I'm talking with my Japanese friend.

일본인 친구와 대화해요.

2. A:What time do you wake up?

______________ 일어나세요?

B: I usually get up at seven.

보통 일곱 시에 일어나요.

3. A: What is your major?

전공이 ____________?

B: My major is Economics.

제 전공은 경제학이에요.

4. A: Who is the president of US now?

지금 ____________ 미국 대통령이에요?

B: The current president is Biden

지금 미국 대통령은 바이든 씨예요.

5. A: If you travel to China, where do you want to visit?

중국에 여행한다면 ____________ 가고 싶어요?

B: I heard Guilin is beautiful.

계림이 아름답다고 들었어요.

6. A: Why do young people want to live in New York City?

젊은 사람들은 _______ 뉴욕에 살고 싶어해요?

B: I think there are a variety of jobs.

다양한 직업들이 많기 때문인 것 같아요.

Activity

Create a roleplay dialogue with your partner.

You want to move to NYC. Call a real estate agent to get information about possible properties to buy/rent. Get as much information as you can.

31

2 Corinthians/고린도후서/哥林多后书/コリント人への手紙第二ー
5:5

Now the one who has fashioned us for this very purpose is God, who has given us the Spirit as a deposit, guaranteeing what is to come.

이런 일을 우리에게 이루어 주시고, 그 보증으로 성령을 우리에게 주신 분은 하나님이십니다.

为此, 培植我们的就是　神，他又赐给我们圣灵作凭据。
Wèi cǐ，péizhí wǒmen de jiùshì　shén，tā yòu cì gěi wǒmen shènglíng zuò píngjù.

わたしたちを、この事(こと)にかなう者(もの)にしては、神(かみ)である。そして、神(かみ)はその保証(ほしょう)として御霊(ごりょう)をわたしたちに賜(たま)わったのである。

Chinese

为此: because of this, ここにおいて [此処に於て], 이 때문에

培植: to cultivate, かなう [叶う], 이루다

赐: to bestow, たまわる [賜(わ)る·給(わ)る], 주시다

凭据: guarantee, ほしょう [保証], 보증

Japanese

事: work, 事 [shì], 일

かな-う [叶う]: to fashion, 培植 [péizhí], 이루다

保証: guarantee, 凭据 [píngjù], 보증

として: as, 作为 [zuòwéi], 으로 (으로 삼아)

御霊: holy spirit, 圣灵 [shènglíng], 성령

賜る: to be given, 领受 [lǐngshòu], 주시다

Korean

이런: this, 这种 [zhèzhǒng], このような

이루다: to achieve, 实现 [shíxiàn], な-す [成す]

보증: guarantee, 凭据 [píngjù], ほしょう [保証]

주시다: to be given, 领受 [lǐngshòu], たまわる [賜(わ)る

Chinese nominalization with 的

Chinese nominalization involves the placement of 的(de) after a word that would otherwise function as a verb. The full structure is attributive+的+noun, as mentioned in Lesson 7. However, when the context is clear, the noun is generally omitted to avoid repetition. i.e. 妈妈买的东西--> 妈妈买的 (what mom has bought) 正在说话的人---> 正在说话的 (the person who is talking)
In this case, the structure of Korean nominalization is verb stem+attributive suffix+것. The attributive suffixes (으)ㄴ 것, 는 것, (으)ㄹ 것 vary depending on the aspects of the verb: (으)ㄴ for a completed action, 는 for an ongoing action, and (으)ㄹ for a prospective action.
こと(for intangible things) and もの(for tangible things) are used in Japanese.

1. I eat whatever my mom makes.

K 저는 어머니가 만드는 것을 다 잘 먹어요.

C 妈妈做的我都吃。

J お母さんが作ったものを食べます。

2. I can't read what you wrote. Please write again.

K 쓴 것을 읽을 수 없네요. 다시 써 주세요.

C 我看不懂你写的。请你再写一遍。

J 書いたのが読めません。もう一度書いてください。

3. Did you understand what the teacher taught today?

K 선생님이 가르친 것을 이해했어요?

C 老师今天上课教的，你都会了吗?

J 今日先生が教えたことが分かりましたか。

When the Chinese 的 is added to the end of the certain commonly used verbs, the verb is transformed into a noun.

吃 --> 吃的 food 먹을 것 食べ物

喝 --> 喝的 drinks 마실 것 飲み物

In addition, when an adjective precedes 的, i.e.大的，小的, it is kind of like saying "the big one" or "the small one" in English. In Chinese the 的 (de) serves the same purpose as the English word "one." By using this pattern, you can avoid repeating the same noun over and over again unnecessarily.

In Japanese, の is used to avoid repeating the same noun.

A: What do you like to eat? 你喜欢吃什么？何が食べたいですか。
뭘 드시고 싶어요?

B: Sweet (food). 甜的。甘いものです。단 것이요.

A: What kind of boyfriend are you looking for? 你想找一个什么样的男朋友？どんな彼氏を探しているんですか。어떤 남자친구를 찾으세요?

B: A tall and handsome one. 又高又帅的。背が高くてハンサムな人です。키가 크고 잘 생긴 사람이요.

A: Do you like the black T-shirt or the red one? 你喜欢黑的T恤还是红的？ 黒いTシャツがいいですか。それとも、赤いのですか。 까만 티셔츠가 좋으세요? 빨간 티셔츠가 좋으세요?

B: The black one. 黑的。 黒いのがいいです。 까만 것이요.

Exercise

Make connections to A and B using the nominalizers.

A: to watch TV, to walk around town listening to music, to wake up in the morning, to be cold, to be difficult, to be a lawyer,...

B: to like, to do every day, to not like, to be normal in winter, to not want, to not say….

Korean benefactive expression ~어/아 주다/드리다

When an action for the benefit of or towards the speaker occurs, the construction action verb + 어/아 + 주다/드리다, is used in Korean. It carries the benefactive meaning '(do) for', where 주다 is plain while 드리다 is humble style.

In Japanese, verbs of giving/receiving are used for this situation. The verbs of giving/receiving verbs are あげる (to give)・もらう (to receive)・くれる (someone gives to me). The polite version is さしあげる・いただく・くださる respectively. For giving and receiving of items, these verbs are used such as プレゼントをプレゼントをあげる・プレゼントをもらう・友達がプレゼントをくれる。verb てform + あげる・もらう・くれる indicates being benefited by someone's action (direct or indirect).

妹にプレゼントを買ってあげるつもりだ。
(I plan to buy a present for my little sister.)
母にセーターの編み方を教えてもらった。
(My mother taught me /I had my mother teach me how to knit a sweater)
友達はビデオの作り方を教えてくれた。
(My friend taught me how to make a video.)

In Chinese, as mentioned in Lesson 6, preposition word 给 is used to introduce the beneficiary or the receiver of the action.

Examples

Now the one who has fashioned us for this very purpose is God.

K 이 일을 우리에게 이루어 주신 분은 하나님이세요.

C 为此，培植我们的就是 神。

J わたしたちを、この事にかなう者にしてくれたのは神である。

1. A: I can't read this email, since it's written in Chinese.

K 중국어로 되어 있어서 이 이메일을 읽을 수 없네요.

C 我读不懂这封邮件，因为它是用中文写的。

J このメールは中国語で書いてあるので、読めません。

B: May I read it for you?

K 제가 읽어 드릴까요?

C 我可以给我你读吗？

J 私が読みましょうか(読んであげましょうか)。

2. A: I took a trip to Maine last summer.

K 지난 여름에 메인에 여행 다녀왔어요.

C 去年夏天我去了缅因州旅游。

J 去年の夏はメインに旅行しました。

B: Really? Can you show me your pictures?

K 그래요? 사진 좀 보여 주세요.

C 真的吗？能给我看你的照片吗？

J そうですか。写真を見せてくれませんか。

Exercise

Translate into each language.

1. May I speak to Steve? (lit. Please change the phone.)
2. Please bring me the book you borrowed.
3. Can you hold this for a moment?
4. I wrote an email for my grandfather.
5. I walked with my friend who asked me to.
6. Thank you for waiting for me.

Activity

Create a telephone conversation between a customer and a pizza store worker.

32

2 Corinthians/고린도후서/哥林多后书/コリント人への手紙第二ー
5:15

And he died for all, that those who live should no longer live for themselves but for him who died for them and was raised again.

그런데 그리스도께서 모든 사람을 위하여 죽으신 것은, 이제부터는, 살아 있는 사람들이 자기 자신들을 위하여 살아가도록 하려는 것이 아니라, 자기들을 위하여서 죽으셨다가 살아나신 그분을 위하여 살아가도록 하려는 것입니다.

并且他替众人死，　是叫那些活着的人不再为自己活，
Bìngqiě tā tì zhòngrén sǐ, shì jiào nàxiē huózhe de rén bù zài wèi zìjǐ huó,
乃为替他们死而复活 的主活。
nǎi wèi tì tāmen sǐ ér fùhuó de zhǔ huó.

そして、彼(かれ)がすべての人(ひと)のために死(し)んだのは、生(い)きている者(もの)がもはや自分(じぶん)のためにではなく、自分(じぶん)のために死(し)んでよみがえったかたのために、生(い)きるためである。

Chinese

并且: and, そして (また), 그리고 (또한)

替: for, ~のために, ~을/를 대신하여

众: all, すべて [総て], 모든

死: to die, しぬ [死ぬ], 죽다

叫: to make, させる, 하도록 하다

不再: no longer, にどと, 다시는

活: to live, いきる [生きる], 살다

乃: so, ここに, 이에

为: for, ために, 위하여

Japanese

すべて: all, 众, 모든

しぬ [死ぬ]: to die, 死, 죽다

いきる [生きる]: to live, 活, 살다

もはや: already, 已经, 벌써

ではなく: not only, 不, ~만이 아니라

よみがえる [蘇る·甦る] : to be raised again, 复活, 다시 살아나다

Korean

그런데: by the way, 可是, しかし

모든: all, 众, すべて

위하여: for, 为, ために

죽다: to die, 死, しぬ [死ぬ]

이제부터는: from now on, これからは, 自此以后

살다: to live, 活, いきる [生きる]

Chinese 不再……了 no longer, なくなる, 더이상~지 않다

When saying an action does not occur any more, the Chinese simply add 不再 before a verb. Usually, particle 了 is used at the end of sentence, unless it is followed by another sentence. In Japanese, なくなる (a combination of a negative form of a verb, adjective, or noun and verb なる). い at the end of the negative form will change to く before the なる. In Korean, the adverb 더이상 (not any more) is put before the negative ending 지 않다.

1. After graduating from high school, I was no longer in touch with him.

C 高中毕业以后，我不再跟他联系了。

K 고등학교를 졸업한 다음에, 그 사람하고는 더이상 연락하지 않았어요.

J 高校を卒業してから、連絡が取れなくなった。

2. My older brother has always been an introvert. After he started working at this company, he was no longer so introverted.

C 我哥哥以前一直是一个很内向的人，进这家公司工作以后，他不再那么内向了。

K 내 형은 이전에 항상 내성적인 사람이었는데 회사에서 일한 후로 더이상 내성적이지 않아요.

J 兄は内向的だった。この会社で働き始めてから、内向的ではなくなった。

3. After getting into a quarrel last week, they were no longer boyfriend and girlfriend.

C 上周吵完架以后，他们不再是男女朋友了。

K 지난 주에 싸운 후로, 그들은 더이상 남자친구 여자친구가 아니에요.

J けんかした後、もうボーイフレンド、ガールフレンドの関係ではなくなった。

Exercises

Explain if anything has changed about you after those events.

1. After graduating from high school, ...

C 高中毕业以后, ________________。

K 고등학교 졸업 이후로, ________________.

J 高校を卒業してから、________________。

2. After starting my first job, ...

C 开始工作以后, ________________。

K 일을 시작한 이후로, ________________.

J 最初の仕事を始めてから、________________。

3. Since I started college, …

C 上大学以来, ________________。

K 대학교에 간 이후로, ________________.

J 大学に入学してから、________________。

4. Since I went to China/Japan/Korea/America, ...

C 去了中国/日本/韩国/美国以后, ________________。

K 중국/일본/한국/미국에 간 후로, ________________.

J 中国/日本/韓国/アメリカに行ってから、________________。

Korean emphasis marker 은/는 것(이다)

은/는 것(이다) is used to put emphasis on an event or a state and

roughly translated as "The thing that~" or "The fact is~". Both 는 and 은 are the noun-modifying suffixes, 는 for present tense verb and 은 for past tense verb and present adjective. 은/는 거예요/거야 is a spoken form.
For this situation, んです・のです is used. This sounds emphatic and used when acknowledging a particular situation or covertly explaining a situation.
In Chinese, this kind of grammar structure does not exist. However, there are many different ways to emphasize a statement. They will be explained in the following chapters.

■ Examples

1. A: What are you doing?

K 뭐 하세요?

C 何をしているんですか。

J 你在做什么？

B: I'm doing my homework. (Lit., It is the thing that I am doing my homework.)

K 숙제하는 거예요.

C 宿題をしているんです。

J 我在做功课。

2. A: What are you watching? (Lit., What is the thing that you are watching?)

K 지금 뭐 보는 거예요?

C 見ているのはなんですか

J 你在看什么？

B: It's a Japanese animation.

K 아~, 일본 애니메이션이에요.

C 日本のアニメです。

J 我在看日本动漫。

3. A: Did you buy a new Macbook?

K 맥북 새로 샀어요?

C 新しいマックブックを買いましたか。

J 你买了新的苹果电脑吗？

B: My parents bought it for my birthday gift. (Lit., It is the thing that my parents bought for my birthday gift.)

K 부모님께서 생일 선물로 사 준 거예요.

C それが両親が買ってくれたんです。

J 是父母送给我的生日礼物。

Exercise

Complete the conversation pairs using 은/는 거예요.

1. A: Are you going to the library even on weekends?

K 주말에도 공부하러 도서관에 가세요?

J 週末に図書館へ行くんですか。

C 你连周末都去图书馆吗？

B: ______________________________ I have an exam next Monday. (Lit., It is the thing that I have an exam on next Monday.)

2. A: What do people do in a long line?

K 사람들이 줄을 길게 서서 뭐 해요?

J 列に並んで何をしているんですか。

C 大家在排队等什么？

B: ______________________________ They are waiting in line to get the Coronavirus vaccine. (What people are waiting for is to get the Coronavirus vaccine.)

3. A: What is Qipao?

K 치파오가 뭐예요?

J 旗袍は何ですか

C 旗袍是什么？

B: ______________________________ It is worn by Chinese women.

4. A: What is Yutnori?

K 윷놀이가 뭐예요?

J ユンノリは何ですか。

C Yutnori是什么？

B: ______________________ It is played by Korean people on New Year's day.

5. A: What is Natto?

K 낫또가 뭐예요?

J 納豆は何ですか。

C 纳豆是什么？

B: ______________________ It is eaten by Japanese people.

Activity

Explain objects from each culture using 는/은 거예요.

33

2 Corinthians/고린도후서/哥林多后书/コリント人への手紙第二ー
5:17

Therefore, if anyone is in Christ, the new creation has come: The old has gone, the new is here!

누구든지 그리스도 안에 있으면, 그는 새로운 피조물입니다. 옛 것은 지나갔습니다. 보십시오, 새 것이 되었습니다.

若有人在基督里，他就是新造的人，旧事已过，
Ruò yǒurén zài jīdū lǐ, tā jiùshì xīnzào de rén, jiùshì yǐguò,
都变成新的了。
dōu biàn chéng xīn dele.

だれでもキリストにあるならば、その人(ひと)は新しく(あたらしく)造(つく)られた者(もの)である。古(ふる)いものは過(す)ぎ去(さ)った、見(み)よ、すべてが新(あたら)しくなったのである。

Chinese

若: if, もし [若し], 만약

有: there be, ある, 있다

就: that is (to say), すなわち, 곧

新: new, あたらし-い [新しい], 새롭다

造: to make, つくる [造る], 만들다

旧: old, ふるい [古い·旧い], 옛

事: event, こと [事], 일

已: already, もう, 이미

过: to pass, すぎる [過ぎる], 지나가다

变成: to change into, かわる[変わる], 변하다

Japanese

だれでも: whoever, 无论是谁, 누구든지

その人: that person, 他, 그 사람

新しい: new, 新, 새롭다

造る: to make, 造, 만들다

者: man, 人, 사람

古い: old, 旧, 옛

もの: man, 人, 사람

過ぎる: to pass, 过, 지나다

さる [去る]: to leave, 去, 떠나다

みる [見る] : to look, 見, 보다

Korean

누구든지: whoever, 无论是谁, だれでも

안에: inside, 里, うら [裏]

있다: to be, 有, ある

새롭다: new, 新, 新しい

피조물: creation, 被造物 [bèizàowù], ひぞうぶつ [被造物]

옛: old, 旧, 古い

것: thing, …的东西, もの [物]

지나가다: to pass by, 过去, 過ぎる

보다: to look, 見, みる [見る]

되다: to become, 成为, なる [為る]

Position words in Chinese, Korean and Japanese

In Chapter 13, we learned how to indicate the location of an object with the Chinese complement 在, Japanese あります(for inanimate objects), います (for living things), and Korean 이 있다. In this lesson, we will learn the basic position words in each language.

Above, on	Below, under	Left	Right	Front
上(面) shàngmian	下(面) xiàmian	左(边) zuǒbian	右(边) yòubian	前(面) qiánmian
上	下	左	右	前
위	아래	왼쪽	오른쪽	앞

Back, behind	Next to	Middle	Inside	Outside
后(面) hòumian	旁边 pángbiān	中间 zhōngjiān	里(面) lǐmian	外(面) wàimian
後ろ	となり	間	中	外
뒤	옆	사이	가운데	밖

Note that in Chinese, position words are sometimes followed by 边 or 面. However, when the location broadly encompasses an area such as a city or country, i.e. in China, 里(面) is not used. The phrase is simply 在中国.

1. A: Where is my book?

K 내 책이 어디에 있어요?

C 我的书在哪儿？

J 私の本はどこにありますか。

B: It's on the desk.

K 책상 위에 있어요.

C 在桌上。

J 机の上にあります。

2. A: Where's your teacher?

K 선생님은 어디 계세요?

C 你的老师在哪儿？

J 先生はどこにいますか。

B: She's in the front of the classroom.

K 교실 앞에 계세요.

C 她在教室的前面。

J 教室の前にいます。

3. A: Where's the library?

K 도서관이 어디에 있어요?

C 图书馆在哪儿？

J 図書館はどこにありますか。

B: It's next to the cafeteria.

K 식당 옆에 있어요.

C 在餐厅的旁边。

J 食堂のとなりにあります。

4. A: Where should I meet you?

K 어디에서 만날까요?

C 我在哪儿跟你见面？

J どこで会いましょうか。

B: How about outside the classroom?

K 교실 밖에서 만나는 것 어때요?

C 在教室外面，怎么样？

J 教室の前はどうですか。

Activity

1. Ask your partner where the following object or place is.

A: ________ 在哪儿？

B: ________ 在 ________ +position word

钱包 wallet

电脑 computer

宿舍 dorm

学生餐厅 student's cafeteria

健身房 gym

2. Name an object from the image, and then describe where it is based on its relative location.

Japanese conditional ば

The Japanese conditional ば（S1 ば、S2）translates to "only if", or "in order for the situation described in S2 to be realized, the situation in S1 must to happen." In that sense, its usage is not as versatile as another conditional たら.

Since there is no conjugation in Chinese, the adverb 就 is used to connect the first conditional clause and the second clause indicating the result.

The Korean conditional, in this case, corresponds to the ending 다면/라면 attached to the verb or adjective stem.

Verbs

- Affirmative:

  たべる(ru) → たべれば(reba)

  のむ (mu) → のめば (meba)

  くる (ru) → くれば(reba)

- Negative:

  たべない → たべなければ

  のまない → のまなければ

  こない → こなければ

Adjectives

- i-adjectives:

  おおきい → おおきければ

  おおきくない → おおきくなければ

- na-adjectives:

  べんり → べんりなら(ば)

  べんりじゃない → べんりじゃなければ

Nouns

学生 → 学生なら(ば)

学生じゃない → 学生じゃなければ

1. If I just rest a bit, then I will feel better.

K 조금만 쉰다면 좋아질 거예요.

C 我休息一会儿就会感觉好一点。

J 少し休めば楽になります。

2. If you take medicine, it will heal.

K 약을 먹는다면 나을 거예요.

C 你吃药，就会好。

J 薬を飲めば治ります。

3. If you leave the house now, you will make it.

K 지금 떠난다면 만날 수 있어요.

C 你现在出门就能准时到。

J 今家を出れば間に合います。

4. Even if you don't go to the library, you will find out if you look it up on the Internet.

K 도서관에 가지 않아도, 인터넷으로 찾는다면 알수 있어요.

C 即使你不去图书馆，也能在网上查到。 就

J 図書館に行かなくても、インターネットで調べれば分かります。

The resultant clause cannot be a command, request, invitation, wish or expression of intention if an action verb is used in the conditional clause.

5. If I go to Kyoto, I want to stay at a Japanese inn.

要是我去京都，我想住在一个日式旅馆。

× もし京都に行けば、りょかんにとまりたいです。

○ もし京都に行ったら、りょかんにとまりたいです。

○ 교토에 가면, 료칸에 머물고 싶어요.

○ 교토에 간다면, 료칸에 머물고 싶어요.

6. If Yamada-san is in, please have him come over here.

要是山田先生在，请让他来这里。

○ 山田さんがいらっしゃれば、来てもらってください。

○ 야마다씨가 온다면 여기에 오게 하세요.

○ 야마다씨가 오면 여기에 오게 하세요.

7. If we are not sure about how to get there, let's ask someone.

要是我们不知道怎么到那里，就问一下别人。

○ 道が分からなければ、だれかに聞きましょう。

○ 길을 모른다면, 사람들한테 물어봅시다.

○ 길을 모르면, 사람들한테 물어봅시다.

8. If the apartment is not too expensive and it is clean, I will buy it.

要是公寓不太贵，也很干净，我就买。

○ アパートが高くなくてきれいならば、買うつもりです。

○ 아파트가 비싸지 않다고 깨끗하다면, 제가 살게요.

Exercise

Let's give some advice!

1) どうすればテニスが上手になりますか。

(What should I do to get better at tennis?)

2) ペットがあまり食べません。どうすればいいですか。

(My pet doesn't eat much. What should I do?)

3) 寝坊してしまいました。授業の時間まで一時間しかありません。

(I overslept. I only have one hour until my class starts.)

4) 友達とけんかしてしまいました。

(I had an argument with my friend.)

5) ちょっと頭が痛いです。

(I have a bit of a headache.)

6) ______________________________。

memo

memo

memo

memo

망망한 바다 한가운데서 배 한 척이 침몰하게 되었습니다.
모두들 구명보트에 옮겨 탔지만 한 사람이 보이지 않았습니다.
절박한 표정으로 안절부절 못하던 성난 무리 앞에 급히 달려 나온 그 선원이
꼭 쥐고 있던 손바닥을 펴 보이며 말했습니다.
"모두들 나침반을 잊고 나왔기에… "
분명, 나침반이 없었다면 그들은 끝없이 바다 위를 표류할 수 밖에 없을 것입니다.

우리는 삶의 바다를 항해하는 모든 이들을 위하여
그 나침반의 역할을 하고 싶습니다.
우리를 구원하신 위대한 주 예수 그리스도를 널리 전하고 싶습니다.

"하나님은 모든 사람이 구원을 받으며
진리를 아는 데에 이르기를 원하시느니라"
(디모데전서 2장 4절)

Language Triathlon for Peacemakers ❶
피스메이커를 위한 4개 국어 성구 33

지은이 | Dongmin Kim/Jiayi Xu/Kayo Nonaka
발행인 | 김용호
발행처 | 나침반출판사

제1판 발행 | 2023년 1월 5일

등　록 | 1980년 3월 18일 / 제 2-32호
본　사 | 07547 서울특별시 강서구 양천로 583
블루나인 비즈니스센터 B동 1607호
전　화 | 본사 (02) 2279-6321 / 영업부 (031) 932-3205
팩　스 | 본사 (02) 2275-6003 / 영업부 (031) 932-3207
홈　피 | www.nabook.net
이　멜 | nabook365@hanmail.net

일러스트 제공 | 게티이미지뱅크

ISBN 978-89-318-1644-0
책번호 다-3018

값은 뒤표지에 있습니다.